MW00963419

Thunder and Ocean

Shambhala & Buddhism in Nova Scotia

David Swick

Pottersfield Press
Lawrencetown Beach
Nova Scotia, Canada

Canadian Cataloguing in Publication Data

    Swick, David
        Thunder and ocean
        ISBN 1–895900–00–X
    1. Buddhist sects — Nova Scotia. 2. Vajradhatu (Association).
    I. Title.
    BQ749.N62S94   294.3'923'09716   C96–950139–0

Cover design: Cat & Mouse Creative Services, Halifax, N.S.
Cover illustrations: Sue Klabunde
Cover photo: Robin Johnston

Pottersfield Press gratefully acknowledges the ongoing support of the Nova Scotia Department of Education, Cultural Affairs Division, as well as the Canada Council and the Department of Canadian Heritage.

Printed in Canada

Pottersfield Press
Lawrencetown Beach
RR 2 Porters Lake
Nova Scotia, Canada

Contents

Acknowledgements

Whycocomagh? and *Afterthought* originally appeared in *First Thought Best Thought* by Chogyam Trungpa, 1983. Reprinted by arrangement with Shambhala Publications, Inc., 300 Massachusetts Avenue, Boston, MA 02115.

Halifax originally appeared in *Warrior Songs* by Chogyam Trungpa, published by Trident Publications, Halifax, Nova Scotia, 1991. 1991 Diana J. Mukpo. All rights reserved. Used by permission of the publisher.

Farewell to Boulder originally appeared in *Royal Songs* by Chogyam Trungpa, published by Trident Publications, Halifax, Nova Scotia, 1995. 1995 Diana J. Mukpo. All rights reserved. Used by permission of the publisher.

Merrier than the Maritimes is used by permission. 1994 Diana J. Mukpo.

The edited excerpt from a talk by Chogyam Trungpa following his second trip to Nova Scotia in 1979 is from an unpublished manuscript, all rights reserved. Used by permission of Diana J. Mukpo.

Excerpts from a talk by Chogyam Trungpa, given to an international meeting of representatives of the Shambhala Buddhist community are from an unpublished manuscript, all rights reserved. Used by permission of Diana J. Mukpo.

Introduction

Thunder, to the Buddhist mind, is good news. A cracking, booming sky is a heavenly dragon proclaiming powerful, irrefutable truth. The symbolism goes further: every time someone experiences a flash of waking up to reality, it's accompanied by a thunderclap of awareness.

Ocean, for Nova Scotians, means much more than sustenance and transportation. It provides definition. No Nova Scotian lives more than fifty miles from the sea, and the great majority hug the coast.

Thunder and ocean, traditions of the Far East and east coast of Canada, come together in modern Nova Scotia.

I am not a Buddhist, nor a Shambhalian, but I am a Nova Scotian. I first met members of the Shambhala community through my work as editor of the arts section, and more recently as a daily columnist with *The Halifax Daily News*. Usually I found them to be decent and thoughtful, but then I kept hearing rumours — of wealth, wild living, and weapons training. As to what they actually believed and practiced, I couldn't say.

A number of people offered suggestions, advice, and support in the writing of *Thunder and Ocean*. They include Ken Swick, Stewart Young, Lesley Choyce, Stephen Kimber, and Joe and Fran Melvin. The research departments of the Halifax Main Branch and Saint Mary's University libraries were, as always, energetic and professional. The Cultural Affairs Division of the Department of Education helped out with a grant. Doug MacKay and Bill Turpin of *The Halifax Daily News* offered editorial comments and unequivocal support. All of this is deeply appreciated.

The Shambhala community has been generous with time and attention. I want to thank Carolyn Gimian, Shari Vogler, Molly De Shong, Jan Watson, and Judith Smith, all in Halifax; my brother Steve Swick and Anne Bruce in Vancouver; and Dan Hessey and Alyn Lyon in Colorado. Professional photographers Marvin Moore, Diana Church, and John Sherwood were kind to allow me use of their fine work.

This book was edited by Tim Carlson, a talented journalist and writer. It made the leap from concept to reality thanks to the strength and patience of Robin Johnston. Sometimes, her belief in this project surpassed my faith.

Thunder and Ocean is written for anyone who wants to know why two ancient Tibetan spiritual traditions now call eastern Canada home — and how all three are faring. It's a fascinating story. For starters, there are different methods of transmitting wisdom. Both Tibetan traditions are passed on by learned teachers. In Nova Scotia, the best of what we are, we learn from our grandmothers.

For my grandmothers,

Miriam Melvin
and
Nancy Swick

We shall not cease from exploration,
and the end of all our exploring
will be to arrive where we started
and know the place for the first time.
                              — *T.S. Eliot*

Work out your own salvation with diligence.
                              — *Gautama the Buddha*

Wherever you go, that's where you are.
                              — *Nova Scotia blues legend Dutch Mason*

Chapter 1

They Came From Away

May is Nova Scotia's most disappointing month. Spring fails to give way to summer; trees remain leafless. While the rest of the continent basks in a relief of fine weather, Nova Scotians brave a month of unfulfilled promise.

Yet it was a ten-day province-wide car tour, in rainy and cold May 1977, that opened the door to the most unlikely immigration ever to land in Nova Scotia. It would result in profound changes in the lives of thousands of people — both in the province and "come-from-aways." Out traversing the province's highways was a three-car entourage of ten people, led by the Prince of Bhutan.

At least, that's who he said he was. Chogyam Trungpa, Rinpoche, had selected Nova Scotia to be world headquarters of his Tibetan Buddhist organization, Vajradhatu International. He was travelling the chosen province as a prince for several reasons: in his home region of Tibet he was honored with regal titles, he was a close friend of the Royal Family of Bhutan, he wanted a designation fitting the occasion and, most of all, he thought it would be fun. Accompanying Trungpa were some of his most trusted friends and advisors. All had been directed not to tell anyone where they were going. For now, it would be their secret.

Nova Scotia is not a place people pass through on the way to somewhere else. Physically isolated, it juts out of eastern Canada into the North Atlantic. The weather can be frightful.

9

The license plates sport a tourism slogan — Canada's Ocean Playground — but neglect to mention that the water is usually too cold for swimming. Even diehard Bluenosers become distressed by a week-long rainstorm, one hundred hours of fog, or the endless spring which keeps nights freezing into June.

"The whole time it was sort of colorless, that gray kind of color we have here," Jan Watson says. Now co-owner of the Attic Owl Bookstore on South Street in Halifax, at the time she was co-director of the Shambhala community's Karme Choling retreat centre in Vermont.

"So it felt very stony and gray. But I will never forget this woman in Ingonish Beach who opened up her hotel a weekend earlier than usual because we were going to be there. It was a little place, and she was so hospitable and sweet — she got out her mother's silver for us, polished it up and laid on this beautiful spread. There was a lot of that kind of thing."

Which doesn't mean it was fun.

"It was hell," says Watson. "It was really awful. Trungpa wanted royal treatment, so we had to dress and behave accordingly. We dressed for dinner every night, in tails and long clothes and white gloves. I hired a mink stole from Mitchell Furs for the week. It was bizarre: we were sort of pretending to be lords and ladies, which we weren't, really. And it rained all the time."

The trip started poorly and got worse. "At the start he was not happy — he was very black. This would happen to him very occasionally and was always terrifying. He would sort of withdraw. I think he was probably going through something quite intense. So initially it was quite difficult, and then we got wetter and colder."

Rarely would the group stay in a town for more than one night. They would check into a hotel, have dinner, and the next morning get back in the cars and drive some more. In the capital city of Halifax the party stayed at the Lord Nelson Hotel, and went to dinner at the city's most expensive restaurant, Fat Frank's. The tour proceeded up the Eastern Shore — and took a positive turn the moment they reached Cape Breton Island.

Trungpa was enchanted. "As soon as we crossed the causeway his black mood changed," Watson says, snapping her fingers, "just like that. He started looking around, talking."

Everywhere Trungpa went in Nova Scotia, he was treated royally. Restaurateurs were gracious. Hoteliers offered to sell their properties. The cars drove around Cape Breton Island, then back through Antigonish and Pictou counties and down the centre of the province into the Annapolis Valley. When they pulled up to Wolfville's Old Orchard Inn at the same time as the Apple Blossom Festival queen and her court, the Prince was invited to have his photo taken with the local royalty.

By the time the tour ended, all of Trungpa's companions knew it was beyond questioning. Their community, then numbering about three thousand people, was about to have a new headquarters.

* * *

Nova Scotia as world headquarters of a branch of Tibetan Buddhism? It was an unlikely choice. In 1977 the province was most famous for being provincial. A loyal outpost of the British Empire, it was a proud bastion of Victorian values and Christian faith. Most of the people encountered by Trungpa and his entourage were quietly helping Nova Scotia earn its reputation as Canada's most conservative province. Old money ruled, and little changed. Generations of poverty made mistrust of outsiders key to the provincial character. A small group of families operated just about everything, and the Navy picked up the slack. A weak economy — except in wartime — came to be expected. This in turn fostered lacklustre attitudes including, "It can't be done" and "We might as well accept the way it is."

Nova Scotians were leary of an influx of newcomers professing a "foreign" religion. Some of this fear was habit and some was justified. Buddhism was practically unknown, and religious cults were big news. The Jim Jones Guyana tragedy and the invasion of Antelope, Oregon, by Bhagwan Shree Rajneesh were coming soon.

Yet here was Chogyam Trungpa, a Tibetan Buddhist teacher, out touring the province, preparing to call the place home. He liked the lack of material wealth, the traditions, the low-key dignity. He was pleased, too, that it was not popular enough to be overpopulated — there were fewer than a million people in the whole province. If it wasn't the most exciting place, not on the cutting-edge of modern life, all the better. Nova Scotia, he thought, mixed basic amenities with traditional values and pace. It was a good place to be.

A remarkable path brought Chogyam Trungpa (Rinpoche is a honorific title meaning "precious jewel") to Nova Scotia, winding across cultures, religions, languages, and the world. In his native Tibet he was raised in circumstances both privileged and austere. When he was one year old, Buddhist monks following dreams and other auspicious signs declared him to be an important incarnation, the Eleventh Trungpa Tulku. At age five he entered a monastery to begin his formal education. Sixteen artists and woodcarvers designed his room, painting doors with ornamental flowers and birds, and building shelves to hold his many gifts. Training began daily at five a.m., and included prostrations, memorization and, sometimes, corporal punishment. He became learned in the ancient wisdom of all three schools of Buddhism: hinayana, mahayana, and vajrayana. By the age of nineteen Trungpa was not only head of a number of monasteries, but political overlord of an entire region, leading more than a thousand monks and the peasants who worked the land. Tibet was a religious country: church and state were one. The society's greatest priority was to allow Buddhist teachers to further their understanding of life, death, and the nature of existence.

This infuriated the Communist Chinese, who in 1959 took control of the country. Trungpa — like the Dalai Lama and thousands of other monks — was forced to flee. After a treacherous escape across the Himalayas, Trungpa spent four years in India and six in Britain, before coming to North America in 1970. He travelled the continent teaching, mainly to university students. He suggested they learn to trust themselves rather than spiritual teachers, learn that every moment and thing and person is sacred, and meditate so as to understand the mind's strengths and deceptive powers. When he visited the University of Colorado in Boulder, he was struck by the city's gentle grace and gung-ho American West attitude. Boulder was devoid of big city distractions, and the townsfolk seemed tolerant of outsiders. Not only that, but land was cheap. Trungpa decided to make it his home and centre of operations.

* * *

Just before you enter Boulder, Colorado, there's a scenic lookout. It's worth the stop. Boulder Valley stretches just far and wide enough to be both spacious and cosy. A sweet little city nestles up against a mighty range of Rocky Mountains. Snowcaps glisten.

The city prides itself on being the aerobic capital of the universe, and is home of the herbal tea company Celestial Seasonings. Smoking is not allowed in any public buildings — including the bars. Boulder was immortalized in Stephen King's *The Stand* as the place virtuous people gather for a final, apocalyptic, good-versus-evil battle. Boulder today is sunny, pretty, small, clean, and rich.

Wealthy and hip is a heady mix. The sign on the door of the Boulder Pottery Studio and Gallery indicates a common busy nonchalance. "Open most days about 9 or 10, occasionally as early as 7, but some days as late as 12 or 1. We close about 5:30 or 6, occasionally about 4 or 5, but sometimes as late as 11 or 12. Some days or afternoons we aren't here at all, and lately we've been here just about all the time, except when we're somewhere else, but we should be here then, too! Thanks for stopping — come see us again."

Boulder is a haven of liberalism, the Berkeley of the mountain states. Most U.S. cities are riddled with the stars and stripes;

Boulder has more solar panels than U.S. flags. Favorite bumper stickers include, "Visualize Using Your Turn Signal," "My Son Got Inmate of the Month at Boulder Jail," and "My Kid Sold Drugs to Your Honor Student." In a recent magazine survey, young Boulderites voted their favorite fix for a hangover to be marijuana (beer came second; sleep third). When the wind blows down the mountains, thousands of homes tinkle with the sound of wind chimes.

The early 1970s were a time of spiritual shopping among young people, and everywhere Trungpa spoke he found people eager to become his students. Most were unkempt, hairy, fond of recreational drugs, and profoundly hungry to learn. The keenest of these inevitably moved to Boulder to take a summer course or to live near more Buddhists. By 1979 the city of 75,000 had a Buddhist community of more than 1,500. Not counting children and the university population, one in every twenty-five Boulderites was a Buddhist.

Trungpa's students loved it. Boulder offered spectacular scenery, spiritual searching, and material luxury to boot! What could be better than that?

* * *

Trungpa broke the news about Nova Scotia to his Boulder community in the summer of 1978. He made the announcement before a large audience, and in complete seriousness. But then — he was known for his sense of humour. People looked at each other, incredulous. Could this be true? We're just getting settled here, and he wants to move where? Few had been to Nova Scotia. Most left the meeting thinking Trungpa was probably kidding or would let the idea lapse. He didn't.

The next year a group of thirteen Buddhists settled in Halifax, rented an upstairs office at the corner of Hollis and Sackville Streets, and put an ad in the paper saying meditation instruction was available. It was 1979. There was little response.

The phone may not have been ringing for meditation instruction, but the newcomers did receive some official attention. A provincial government deputy minister, having hired one of the newcomers to work in his office, was startled to receive a phone call from a Canada Customs border guard saying, "I have some Moonies wanting across. They gave your name." Ron Wallace, mayor of Halifax through most of the immigration, says he was "apprehensive" and "mystified as to why they would move here."

When one person moves 3,500 kilometres, over an international border, to a new city, it's an exhausting ordeal. When several hundred people make the same move — for the same reason — it's a phenomenon. From a cautious beginning the Halifax community grew, at first in a trickle, then in a stream.

The newcomers faced practical concerns. The price of houses and apartments seemed exorbitantly high. So did the price of food, what there was of it. You could walk through every grocery store in Halifax and never find an artichoke. The economy was terminally flat, so job prospects were limited. And coming from the U.S. created all kinds of complications. Some were legal. Canadian customs regulations insisted that everyone crossing the border either have a good job, the means to create a business, or private wealth. Many Buddhists who wanted to move were denied a visa, and had to stay in the U.S.A.

After a few years of groundbreaking, Trungpa sent his second-in-command, Osel Tendzin, and most of the board of directors north in 1983, and three years later moved up himself. Between 1986 and 1988, hundreds of Buddhists moved to Halifax. In all, more than five hundred adults landed in the port city. Today, with the dust settled, about four hundred and twenty have taken root in Nova Scotia. The community is changing. No longer is it comprised only of immigrants from the U.S. A couple dozen Europeans and more than one hundred longtime Nova Scotians are now full members as well.

They refer to themselves as the *sangha* (pronounced song-gah), a Sanskrit word meaning community. Eighty per cent of the

Nova Scotia sangha are "old guard," students of Trungpa's from the early days in Colorado. They have studied a variety of Buddhist disciplines, and meditated for thousands of hours. Their conversation is sprinkled with Tibetan and Sanskrit terms — a few might appear in a casual chat. Taste in furnishings and art leans to the Oriental; living quarters often have a spartan elegance.

An overwhelming majority were born and raised American, are white, educated, and upper-middle class. A substantial minority were raised Jewish. Every year more make the commitment of becoming Canadian citizens, but most pay little attention to Canadian politics. CBC Radio is the airwave of choice; *The New York Times* is nearly as popular as the Halifax papers.

Nova Scotians usually refer to "the Buddhists" as if the community thinks and acts as a whole. This is far from the truth — it is a remarkably diverse group of people. There are liberals, conservatives and socialists; teetotalers and drunkards; celibates and sexual dynamos; people of every sexual persuasion; every kind of New Age believer; and all dimensions of cynic. Not all are Buddhists.

Buddhism and Shambhala Training are two distinct disciplines. The former has characteristics usually associated with religion — it offers rules of conduct and a full explanation of the ins and outs of human consciousness. Shambhala is a meditation practice that seems almost tailor-made for our busy age. It focuses on uncluttering the mind, allowing anyone to become more fully awake and alive. Most of the old guard practice both Buddhism and Shambhala, but newer members almost all stay solely with Shambhala Training. Because the entire organization is Shambhala International, the umbrella term that best describes the sangha is: the Shambhala community.

Most members, not surprisingly, have best friends inside the Shambhala community — a result of shared history and interests. Everyone, too, can name someone they dislike. Outside of personal feuds, however, sangha members do tend to help each other. Everyone is issued a list of everyone else; members usually visit the community's medical practitioners, support a variety of community activities for kids, and shop at each other's stores.

"It comes back to Trungpa Rinpoche," Halifax sangha member Michael Scott says. "Because the way he communicated was unique, powerful, and very direct, there's trust. If someone is engaged with his teachings and practicing meditation, there's a connection. It's not like hugs, but it is common ground. Like speaking the same language."

Many sangha members also believe in some forms of energy which in another context would be called New Age. Buddhist astrologers are kept busy preparing personal charts; when moving into a new home or place of business a pan full of juniper is lit on fire, and chanting performed by a parade of people moving through the house to put smoke in every corner. Words to the chant include, "The assembly of the three jewels, the three roots, gods and sages.... To all of those I offer clouds of real and imagined good offerings.... With kindness please grant your blessings."

Despite the monotone chanting, despite the unusual ceremonies and sangha list, the suggestion the group is a cult makes members laugh. It's easy to see why. No two agree on anything. Ask any three a question, and you will receive at least five replies. Views on even the most basic issues vary wildly. Everyone is instructed to trust their own judgment more than any teacher. This is not a group geared to abject devotion.

The one thing members might agree on is the importance of some kind of contemplative practice. Yet even here there is tremendous diversity. Some people are very serious about meditation, are up "practicing" at 6 a.m. daily. Others haven't meditated in months. Some people are at the Shambhala Centre several times a month; others almost never go, and think any focus on the sangha builds a dangerous us/them breach with greater society. Opinions of the founder and Shambhala hierarchy are similarly disparate. Some members revere the ground on which Trungpa Rinpoche marched and stumbled; others are grateful for the inspiration, but think he served the community best with an early exit. In some ways the Shambhala sangha is barely a community at all. They share a significant interest and experiences, but do not necessarily hold any of the same practices or beliefs. First and foremost, it's a collection of individuals.

For all, Trungpa — or his teachings — was the great attraction and remains the glue. Some of the old guard believe the glory days are over: Trungpa was *the* teacher, and today's efforts are a poor attempt to keep his light alive. More, however, believe Trungpa's long-term design is only now coming true.

"Almost everyone in the Halifax Buddhist community were hippies," says Richard John. He first met Trungpa in the early 1970s, after driving his school bus along three hundred miles of California coastline. "Everybody was ready to do anything. Anything! We got into this, and it seemed fantastically radical and profound. Fifteen or twenty years later, we all look like Presbyterians. Everybody has their kids in school, is worried about their job and mortgage, and we're all fifty. There's a kind of normalcy, which is very much the direction Trungpa Rinpoche pushed us in."

Part of that normalcy means opening up to larger society. More than twelve hundred Nova Scotians have taken Shambhala Training. Hundreds more have studied Buddhist philosophy or meditative Nalanda arts including Japanese archery, flower arranging, photography, and calligraphy. At the heart of all of these teachings, practitioners say, is mindfulness, a way to become more fully aware and so live a fuller, more compassionate life.

Community functions take place at the Shambhala Centre, a former Knights of Columbus Hall on Tower Road. The thirty-room Centre houses meeting rooms, a shrine room, and an archive. Upstairs are the offices of Shambhala International, the organization that oversees sangha activities worldwide.

* * *

Why did the Buddhist community move to Nova Scotia? Theories abound. Chogyam Trungpa saw the province in a vision and decided to move, sight unseen. No, he was flying overhead in an airplane, looked down, and was struck with the realization that here was what he was looking for. Or this: Trungpa did a careful measuring of the earth's energy lines, and realized Nova Scotia lies in the crosshairs of an outflow of positive energy.

Despite their own love of the place, most Nova Scotians were not flattered by the immigration. On the contrary, they found it mysterious to the point of suspicion. The newspaper of record, *The Chronicle-Herald*, was particularly agitated, referring to the Buddhists with the loaded term "sect," and sometimes quoting "unnamed sources" speculating about their intentions.

The province has never been a target for mass migration. After the initial European settlement, the next large influx came from the Boston States in the 1770s, British subjects sailing north to stay loyal to the king. Within a few years many decided that the price was too dear, and returned to New England from the province they nicknamed "Nova Scarcity." The great turn-of-the-century migrations that settled western Canada and swelled the nation's largest cities had little impact east of Montreal. Most recently, when a boatload of Sikhs landed on the province's southern coast in 1987, Nova Scotians suffered the indignity of one English-speaking gentleman asking for a taxi to Toronto. Yet suddenly several hundred young, apparently bright, upwardly mobile Americans wanted to move here? Should we be flattered or scared, or both? Why did they come here again?

Nova Scotians weren't the only people asking that question. So too were the Buddhists. Three thousand people throughout the U.S. and Europe were busy looking for difficult answers. Should I quit my job? Uproot my family? Will we like Canada? Will I be able to find work? What if our savings don't last? Why are we doing this again?

Why Nova Scotia? has been a favorite sangha party game for nearly twenty years. Offering one definitive answer was not Trungpa's style. Instead, he offered many answers, most of which fueled the confusion. He made it confusing on purpose —

Trungpa preferred his students find the answers to big questions for themselves.

"The answer I think makes the most sense is: he never thought in the short term," Jan Watson says. "He always thought in the long term. Long, long term. We think maybe ten years is long term, but I think he was thinking in centuries. He felt America would quite soon experience a serious backlash against the openness that was going on in the '60s and '70s, which of course it now is. He thought that trying to establish Buddhism in a strong, long-term way would be very difficult to do in America. But here it would work."

Dana Fabbro is best friend of the present Shambhala community leader, Trungpa's son, Sakyong Mipham Rinpoche. The two were teenagers together in Boulder, and now travel as leader and personal aide. Fabbro lived in Halifax between 1986 and 1990, attending Dalhousie University while working as a waiter at the Soho Kitchen. A polite man with a big smile, he's now in his early thirties.

"I found Halifax a difficult place," he says. "When I first moved here it really kicked me into the ground. I felt like it was my speedy fast mind coming into a place that wasn't speedy and fast. There was a real collision. But this place will always win. It will always win that little battle, because Halifax doesn't go anywhere. It's a very still, simple environment. When you impose your sort of fleeting, hurried mind onto it, it's not going to change. So the mind adapts, and you don't mind waiting in line for an hour while the gals at Sobeys (grocery store) chat about what happened Friday night."

The worst thing about living in Halifax, Fabbro says, is the lack of big city amenities: a wide range of museums and entertainment events.

"But it's such an easy place to just live, simply and basically, and not get caught up in a lot of materialism. Where you live affects how you react to your world emotionally. If you live in New York, you've got to really crank it up. That's the environment. In

Halifax you can turn it down a bit, and it's a precious opportunity. Most Buddhists experience cranking it down through their meditation practice, by going to retreat centres, by removing themselves from distractions. But this is an urban centre where you can live, have a job, and still not get caught up in an habitual, fast-paced track."

"Within our first week here our son, who was ten, asked, 'Why are there so many old people here?'" Jill Scott says. "I said, 'This is normal, this is real life.' Boulder was something else. It's young, fit, hip, white, and for the most part wealthy. It's like living in a Club Med. I like the cultural diversity of Halifax. Here there are ethnic communities. Black people. It's more representative. I thought my kids were lacking that."

Jill and Michael Scott live on Regatta Point, the small, woodsy Northwest Arm peninsula that used to be known as the Edmonds Grounds. She is from New York, he from England. Students of Trungpa Rinpoche's married for more than twenty years, they moved to Halifax in 1986.

Coming from England, Michael Scott was familiar with Nova Scotian characteristics some of his American compatriots found inexplicable.

"When I first visited in 1980 or so the Americans would say things like, 'You think this is North America because the cars are the same and there are McDonalds and so on, but don't be deceived — it's really not. The culture is so different.' I think I tuned into it much more quickly, because of the Englishness of the place: the attitudes, conservatism, lack of flash. For example, people who have money here don't tend to flaunt it. You don't get a lot of conspicuous consumption, although there are people who do have money. And I knew it would take a long time to understand the subtleties."

Jill Scott says that right away she noticed three things about the people of Nova Scotia. "Niceness. Reserve. And the feeling that there was a level at which people would be open to you, and then another place — intimacy — that takes longer. In the U.S.

people are intimate very quickly. They tell you everything about their lives in the first conversation. They don't spare you any details! It's very different here. I worked on the PTA at my elementary school, and felt really comfortable and liked everybody, but friendship only goes so far. It's hard to become good friends — it takes longer. This place reminds me of growing up in the Bronx in the fifties. I grew up in a neighbourhood where I had aunts and uncles on the next block. My kids have friends here whose grandparents live on the next block. I was happy to bring my children to a place where this was still happening. In Boulder, everybody was from away."

Michael Scott says Nova Scotia has a surprising lack of class or wealth restriction. "A well-established stockbroker said to me, 'You know, Michael, you can do anything you want here. You can enter this society at any level, depending on your interests, your background, and your abilities.' There's a porousness here — I haven't found a sense of doors closed. You can call the senior person in practically any sphere and say, 'I'm so and so, somebody suggested I give you a call. Can we get together and have lunch?' Then you sit down and you can talk. I've found that again and again. In that way, it's very open."

If Nova Scotia is less materialistic than most of North America, it might be because it has less material wealth. One of money's most unsavory powers is its ability to beget a need for more. Most Nova Scotians value a number of things more than money: family; friends; the community where they live. It is not a society that places money above everything else.

"I don't feel like anybody here gets really serious about materialism," Michael Scott says. "I mean, people want things. But people are remarkably ungreedy. It's extremely decent. Unusually decent. Visitors comment on this. You walk down the street and people say 'Nice day!' and actually mean it! This has to do with genuineness. And that's the connection that attracted Trungpa Rinpoche."

"In one sense this is a sort of insignificant place, so there's room for something good," Jan Watson says. "Tibet is not the place anymore — Trungpa said a number of times that the West is the place for Buddhism now. It had its day in the East. The new blood of it, the resurgence of it, with the real genuineness and strength and benefit of it, has to be somewhere else. And the West is the place.

"He wanted to find somewhere isolated yet accessible, where it could take root for a long time. He started thinking about it in 1975. In the fall of 1975 he was asking people, 'Where would be such a place?' There was an Englishman called David Darwent, who had been to Halifax as a sailor. So had Marty Janowitz (from 1990-96 executive director of the Clean Nova Scotia Foundation). Marty and he both suggested this place. A lot of other places were suggested also — Bermuda, New Zealand, some Pacific islands, more romantic and warm places.

"James George was the Canadian ambassador to India at the time Rinpoche was coming out of Tibet. They met, had an immediate friendship, and corresponded intermittently over the years. Before he finally decided on Nova Scotia, Rinpoche said, 'I need to have an external influence somehow confirm that Nova Scotia is the right place.' Shortly after that he got a letter from James George talking about a lot of ecological things, Tibetan refugees and so on, and in a sort of aside he said something about Nova Scotia being a safe place. And Rinpoche said, 'That's it.'"

Even among Buddhists who decided not to move north, Nova Scotia enjoys a reputation as a sane place to be.

"Trungpa thought Nova Scotia was a good place because people would be allowed to practice without huge distraction," says Dan Hessey, director of development at the Rocky Mountain Shambhala Centre in Colorado. "It's about creating an environment. There they could grow, get stronger, and therefore reach out to other people. There's something basically good about the people of Nova Scotia. They are not corrupted by the virus in the West that infects everything we touch. The Western world says: that gentle, quiet, good thing that is the way we bring up our kids, that attaches people to a place, that can barely be named — it doesn't exist. It can be bought and sold. Yet Nova Scotians know it exists, and it is not for sale.

"Nova Scotia is good, too, because no one just passes through there. Tibet was good because it was on the Silk Route, and so they'd hear a bit of various cultures and could pick and choose what they wanted in. Nova Scotia is protected by being far from any place else. Plus it has weather that will never invite anybody. Colorado gets three hundred days of sun and glorious weather; Nova Scotia will never do that. Colorado attracts people for the wrong reasons. It's a beautiful, easy place to be. Trungpa called Nova Scotia a hard, tough place to be. He was thinking it would help people stay focused."

* * *

The Buddhists refused entrance by Canada Customs would miss out on a gentle revolution. Just as the sangha began to arrive, Nova Scotia was beginning to change. Culturally, socially, and politically, the province was starting to throw off its dusty coat. More and more Nova Scotians were travelling, and coming home with ideas on how to keep the best of provincial tradition, while infusing it with what could be. There was a growing awareness of how much there is to be proud of, and how special the province is.

Self-confidence was inspired by local artists' talent and success. Homegrown music had always been popular, but in the late 1970s Dutch Mason, the Minglewood Band, and Buddy and the Boys enjoyed superstar status *and* the backing of a fledgling music industry. Regional talent was encouraged by television and CBC Radio. Local movies and the best films in the world were being shown at the newly-opened Wormwood's Dog & Monkey Repertory Cinema in Halifax. Red Herring Co-operative Bookstore was launched, bringing to the province thousands of books the chain stores would never provide. *New Maritimes* magazine hit newsstands in 1981, establishing a new standard for investigative journalism. Students of the Nova Scotia College of Art and Design and the city's universities started staying in town after graduation. The black, poor, and gay and lesbian communities began to demand respect. The province was waking up.

The Shambhala community added confidence and energy to this coming of age. Concentrated in Halifax County, but with small groups in Cape Breton, Lunenburg County, and Annapolis Royal, sangha members have introduced new ways of seeing, eating, teaching, and staying well. They have directed the Clean Nova Scotia Foundation, the Atlantic Film Festival, Symphony Nova Scotia, and the Nova Scotia Sea School. The province's largest health food store, Great Ocean, is owned by these newcomers, as is the Italian Market, Paradise Bakery, and the trendsetting Trident Cafe. Sangha members are psychiatrists, craftspeople, teachers, film-makers, entrepreneurs, media, and health professionals. If Nova Scotians want to take a dance lesson, enrol a child in acting, buy pottery, get a therapeutic massage, or bite into an organic apple, chances are there's a sangha member nearby.

Twenty years after his father first toured the province, the present leader of Shambhala International, Sakyong Mipham Rinpoche, says the choice of Halifax as world headquarters was emphasized with Trungpa's final breath.

"He chose to die here," the sakyong says. "He didn't want the community to be essentially an American community, he was trying to make it more universal. It almost took his death to bring people here. Nova Scotia is good. He felt something here, some sort of connection. Knowing him, he had some auspicious signs: from both the Buddhist and Shambhala points of view, all elements have deities. And I think our community has helped here, contributed in a positive way. You want a place you can influence. After twenty years in Boulder, well, we were just another thing. In America it's this thing one week, the next week it's that thing. He was not satisfied with Boulder. It was too easy, people became lazy quickly."

* * *

Trungpa talked about his choice of headquarters in 1979, at a community meeting in Lake Louise, Alberta. At that point he had visited Nova Scotia twice — on the ten-day car journey in 1977, and on another brief visit in April, 1979.

"When I first landed in Nova Scotia, I couldn't touch the ground even — it felt too shaky," Trungpa said. "This time I stepped out on the road, knelt down and felt the soil — a slightly papal approach maybe: feeling the earth. It was a well-paved road — still, it felt very good: gentleness coming through my palms, inviting and good. The psychological mentalities of a place are affected by weather, of course. We will take that into account, but we could extend that logic — even if there is severe weather, we still could feel goodness with our palms. So it was a very grounding experience. Very moving, although outside of the airport it wasn't moving. I was very moved nonetheless. Very good and real.

"You can't feel this anywhere else — except that I would feel the same thing if I went back to Tibet and touched the side of a mountain, but I never had such an experience outside of Tibet before. Throughout our journey, I found the island (Nova Scotia) is connected with Tibet...

"There doesn't seem to be any resistance as far as the psychic level, and the people are very cooperative. In fact, they seem to be starved and need some further energy to be put on them. I felt a general sense of longing for something else to happen. I checked several times, maybe a hundred times when we were here. I looked to see if this sense was my own invention or actually happening. My conclusion was that it is happening on the ground itself.

"We dealt with the local people and they seemed to have some kind of understanding. I would talk to people around us —

they were not shocked at all, but very pleased we're there — somewhat perplexed, of course, at who we are, but nevertheless very pleased.

"We visited this little home in Antigonish — the gentleman was very pleased to have us. We arrived there and Mr. Perks happens to say 'Your Highness.' The gentleman said, 'We have royalty here?' After that the energy changed completely. He began to offer us beer, scotch, and anything from their house. We were buying a kilt from him. The energy was very clean cut. He had never heard of Tibet. Couldn't care less. 'Prince from where?' Tibet. Couldn't care less.

"But our presence was enough to acknowledge that we mean genuine connection — connected to dollars maybe, but still a general sense of natural openness. A similar sense is the little tree we brought back (to Colorado) from Nova Scotia — it is responding so well. It was snatched from its homeland but still surviving."

Still, for most of his students Nova Scotia took some getting used to. The miserable weather, the geographical isolation, the poor economy, and lack of amenities took a toll. Some of the earliest settlers struggled with a desire to get out. Trungpa addressed this at a 1984 Halifax talk by confirming his choice and urging the sangha to embrace the challenge.

"Personally, I regard this particular location, province, as a sacred place," he said. "That's why we are trying to establish our society here. It is also very beautiful, and it is highly workable. That is not in the American sense; it's not like Florida. You might have to relate with reality much more so than you have ever had to...

"Don't give up. Instead, give *in*, fully, thoroughly. We do need some kind of discipline. And your disciplinarian is going to be myself. I will be watching everybody who comes into this province. And I will make you work harder, practice further, more than on American land. As I said already, you are not in Florida, or California, because this place is worth cultivating and worth working with."

By "establish a society here" Trungpa did not mean a hostile takeover or insidious saturation. Proseletyzing is not the Shambhala style. His aim was not so much to multiply the sangha size as to ensure present members would be in a good place to practice, among gentle neighbours. To Trungpa's mind the people of Nova Scotia and the Shambhala community share a profound and rare value: a belief in human dignity.

* * *

One of Trungpa Rinpoche's most popular talks, later articulated in *Cutting Through Spiritual Materialism* (Shambhala Publications) is about the six realms of being. A staple of Tibetan Buddhist teaching, the realms are understood to be psychological states, worlds we create with our own minds.

Once you achieve a major goal in life — get married, win a job, become a parent — insecurities can begin to fall away. If you have everything you aspired to, Trungpa would say, you are in heaven, God Realm. Things feel so good, in fact, that you just might start to dwell on your achievements and ignore anything deemed unpleasant. As a result, you become blissful and proud.

Sooner or later, reality steps up to let the air out of the balloon. The ego cannot keep up the illusion of permanent bliss. So you feel vulnerable again, confused and threatened, and fall into the Realm of the Jealous Gods. You become filled with anxiety, envy, and all kinds of worries. You want that godlike feeling back, try to figure out what has gone wrong, and become fixated with finding a solution. So you return to the powers of intellect. The Human Realm.

Human intelligence is great for many things, but when it tries to find the way back to the God Realm, the result is suffering and confusion. You wind up beaten and exhausted, in Animal Realm, where you simply plod along, following usual behaviour patterns. You become deaf and dumb to anything that might challenge a narrow world view.

Eventually, though, nostalgia for a better life breaks through and the hunger for something better begins to grow. The hunger grows and grows, to a point where you begin to aggressively seek what you want — and fall into Hungry Ghost Realm. From there, it's a short drop to a life filled with anger, wanting, and desperation. You find yourself in Hell.

Once you hit the depths of Hell, naturally, you rebound, and start moving up the ladder towards God Realm. Trungpa suggested that we are always on the move, trapped in conceptual worlds the mind creates — worlds in which each phase seems real and solid and permanent, not just a creation of mind.

The good news is that one realm offers a way to break free from the otherwise never-satisfied cycle. The Human Realm. Human intellect, our ability to discriminate, gives us the power to question the whole struggle. Rather than simply following our hunger and pride, rather than believing that every world we experience is solid, we have a choice.

Not just people go through these levels. Nations do. Families do. So do cities and provinces.

"Trungpa wanted a place where the teachings could grow and people could practice," Dan Hessey says. "Having a sympathetic environment is extremely helpful. If you went to New York it would be difficult. Big cities are in Hungry Ghost Realm, are full of speed and hunger and aggression. The atmosphere is one of people always hungry to have something more: a Mercedes, more money, whatever. If you went to Bosnia to practice it would even be harder — there is too much agony and pain. It's Hell Realm. Those environments make it harder for something good to grow.

"Human Realm is the only one of the six realms of human experience where people can be good to each other. So the realm people want to be in is Human Realm. But you can't be there unless you're in a space where basic goodness can thrive. War zones won't do it. Rich cities won't do it. Nova Scotia does it. In order for the plant to be strong enough to function in New York City and other places, the root has to be in Nova Scotia."

Chapter 2

The Key

He was a holy fool, a crazy saint, a visionary, and a drunk. He was a scholar, a comedian, a poet, and a brilliant teacher. He loved to tickle feet. Chogyam Trungpa, Rinpoche, was fiercely intelligent, miraculously insightful, playful, moody, and tough. He was notoriously late, inspired respect and fear, and was the first Tibetan ever to become a British subject. He sometimes fell asleep while meditating.

Trungpa was all this and more. A painter, poet, playwright, and photographer, a master of calligraphy and flower arrangement, he authored more than twenty books, including *Shambhala: The Sacred Path of the Warrior*, which has sold more than 250,000 copies. Raised in the East, he became a spiritual leader of Westerners, founding more than a hundred meditation and retreat centres in North America and Europe.

"Trungpa is key," says Halifax sangha member Michael Scott. "It was the way he related to us, and to Nova Scotia, which explains what we're doing here. His genius was to be able to communicate in the idiom of whoever he was talking to... and not just about the teachings. It has to do with genuineness. He was genuine.

"Most of us are lucky enough to have had one or two great teachers. Maybe in English or math, maybe in high school. Great teachers, who really communicate. If a teacher shows you insight, he's got you. Because what he's saying is true, and you can't deny it. Trungpa Rinpoche had that, on a vast scale, only he taught how the human mind works...

"Why would all these people come to Nova Scotia? It defies logic. I'm a pretty skeptical person — I wouldn't expect I'd do it! It has to do with these qualities."

* * *

The man who would lead hundreds of people to modern Halifax was born into primitive circumstances. Chogyam Trungpa saw his first movie when he was fifteen, and didn't ride in a car until he was nineteen years old. His mother could never have predicted what the future would hold — how much the secluded world of Tibet would change, and where her son would go to teach.

Things started normally enough, in a medieval sort of way. Trungpa was born in February 1939 in Geje, a small tent village on a high plateau in northeastern Tibet. The villagers lived as they had for centuries, in yak hair tents they would pick up and move with their livestock. His mother, Tungtso-drolma, had experienced a traumatic pregnancy. While carrying Trungpa, Tungtso-drolma's husband left her and a baby daughter. By the time her son was born she had remarried and was working for relatives, doing chores including milking the yaks.

It was a propitious birth, during the Tibetan New Year festival, on the day of a full moon, February 3 or 4. The child was born in a cow shed. He was given the names Chokyi Gyatso, meaning Ocean of Dharma (Ocean of the Buddhist teachings); his last name was Mukpo, the name of his clan. (Tibetans use names differently than the English-speaking world, and often abbreviate them; as an adult in the West he would take the first part of his given names to come up with Chogyam, and added his incarnate, Trungpa.)

In his 1966 autobiography, *Born in Tibet* (Shambhala Publications), Trungpa said both his conception and birth were accompanied by remarkable events. "The night of my conception, my mother had a very significant dream that a being had entered her body with a flash of light; that year flowers bloomed in the neighbourhood although it was still winter, to the surprise of the inhabitants... On (the day I was born) a rainbow was seen in the village, a pail supposed to contain water was unaccountably found full of milk, while several of my mother's relations dreamt that a lama was visiting their tents."

The lama would come soon enough. The year before Trungpa's birth, an important Buddhist monk had died — the tenth incarnation of the Trungpa Tulku, the supreme abbot of the Surmang group of monasteries. Tibetan Buddhists have believed in tulkus — enlightened beings who voluntarily return to human form in order to teach others the path out of suffering — since the twelfth century. Some months after the death of the tenth Trungpa Tulku the XVI Gyalwa Karmapa, head of one of the four schools of Tibetan Buddhism, had two visions suggesting where to find the eleventh. He sent three monks off to find him. It took five days to get to Geje; the monks made a list of the one-year-old children and left. Looking over the list, Gyalwa Karmapa realized they had only taken names of the babies of important families. He sent them back a second time.

The village, meanwhile, had changed locations, moving to higher ground. There the monks found a family that fit the vision. They were in a tent facing south, had a one-year-old boy and a big red dog. But there was some confusion over names. Gyalwa Karmapa had dreamt of the biological father of the child, not his present parent. Helping settle the issue was Trungpa himself. "They looked closely at the baby, for as soon as he had seen them in the distance he waved his little hand and broke into smiles as they came in," Trungpa writes. "So the monks felt that this must be the child, and gave him the gifts which Gyalwa Karmapa had sent, the sacred protective cord and the traditional scarf; this latter the baby took and hung round the monk's neck in the prescribed way, as if he had already been taught what was the right thing to do; delighted, the monks picked me up, for that baby was myself, and I tried to talk."

A miraculous birth. Gifts sent by a wise man to an infant child born in a cattle shed. Christianity does not have a monopoly on miraculous births, of course; many religions through millennia have reported miraculous births. But the similarities are remarkable, and things get more extraordinary from there.

"My earliest memory is being in a room with several monks who were talking to me, and I was answering them. I was later told that my first words were Om Mani Padme Hum; probably, I did not say them very correctly."

It was decided that the child whose first words were an ancient mantra would be sent to live near a monastery immediately. His mother would go too, and look after him until he was five; his stepfather stayed in Geje. The baby was brought to a monastery and given a test. Several pairs of objects were presented, including walking sticks and rosaries. In each case he picked out the one that had belonged to the tenth Trungpa Tulku.

The enthronement of the eleventh Trungpa Tulku took place in front of a large assembly. Gyalwa Karmapa cut the child's hair to symbolize a cutting away from the material and an entering into the spiritual life. A monastery regent sat on a throne with Trungpa in his lap, and spoke all of his responses.

"From today I take refuge in the Buddha.

"From today I take refuge in the Dharma.

"From today I take refuge in the Sangha."

"At the moment when he put the scissors to my hair there was a clap of thunder, sudden rain, and a rainbow appeared," Trungpa later wrote. "This was thought to be very auspicious... Later that day I was given all the seals and official documents of the tenth Trungpa Tulku. Everyone came to receive my blessing..."

* * *

"The single most important factor of Trungpa Rinpoche's behavior was compassion," Richard John says. "It points to an understanding of compassion that goes way beyond what we think. Usually, we think of Mother Teresa. That's real, but you have to switch gears to see what vajrayana Buddhists mean by compassion.

"It ties into what is a tulku. The idea of a tulku is: if a person undertakes the Buddhist path, and over lifetimes has success, they actually become liberated from ordinary suffering and ordinary confusion. Narrower schools of Buddhism consider that the goal — that's what nirvana means. From the mahayana school on, though, that's not good enough. You have to go beyond your own liberation, and be completely devoted to the benefit of others. Tulkus are liberated beings who deliberately keep manifesting. They have no reason to come back but to benefit others.

"They're still human beings, so they still have their own style. Some are scholarly and traditional and have a small group of students. Trungpa Rinpoche's predecessor was totally his opposite. Totally monastic. Totally strict. He wouldn't ride a horse, because that was too proud. Then you have people at the other extreme, like Trungpa Rinpoche, who just kind of decide they want to inhale the world, and come up with some big scheme.

"You could experience Trungpa Rinpoche's compassion by being in the room. Most of what you would perceive, in the room with him, was a vacuum. There would be this tremendous sense of presence, but there was nothing happening. It was sort of the opposite from our usual experience. Usually there's a lot happening, but no presence. And he wouldn't do anything; he would just be there."

* * *

Trungpa recalled his toddler years as happy. He lived with his mother near the monastery; there were no lessons. When he was three, the Geje village leaders invited Tungtso-drolma to bring the boy back for a visit. She did, with Trungpa riding a white horse that had belonged to his previous incarnation. Villagers were kind, but Trungpa was not allowed to play with other children. Nor was he allowed to take any toys back to the monastery.

He began daily lessons when he was five years old, and his mother went back to their village. Trungpa's first teacher, Asang Lama, had been a student of the tenth Trungpa Tulku. The teacher and student travelled to a retreat centre established by the tenth Trungpa Tulku, built over a cave where the fourth Trungpa Tulku had once spent six years in meditation. It was in a remote spot, on a ledge of high rock, and could only be approached by a long zigzag of steps. There they rose at five a.m. for morning devotions, then breakfast, and reading lessons until noon. After a meal and a thirty-minute rest, they would spend thirty minutes on a writing lesson, and then practice reading until evening. That Trungpa was taught writing was surprising; usually in Tibet children learn to read first, then to write.

The boy received corporal punishment from Asang Lama until age seven. "It was always done with great ceremony," Trungpa later wrote. "After a foreword such as, 'It is like moulding an image; it has to be hammered into shape,' he would prostrate himself three times before me, and then administer the chastisement on the appropriate part."

It was around this age that Trungpa began to have strange dreams. "Though even in pictures I had never seen the things that are made in the West, I dreamt I was riding in a mechanized truck... a few days later in another dream I saw airplanes parked in a field."

Also at seven, Trungpa returned to the monastery and was given a ritual authorization of all the scriptures forming the *Kangyur,* the sayings of the Buddha. This gave him the authority to study, practice and explain their meaning — all one hundred and eight volumes.

The next year Trungpa was ordained as a novice of the Sarvastivadin Order to which most northern Buddhists belong. He was ordained during a full moon, by a monk who had been a student of the tenth Trungpa Tulku. Trungpa then spent three months in retreat, with only his tutor and and a cook. He kept to a strict vegetarian diet and was not allowed outside the retreat centre. There were long hours of meditation and mantras.

Soon Trungpa was to take his Bodhisattva vow when he was eleven years old. This vow, which has been sworn by devout Buddhists for more than two thousand years, including hundreds in Halifax, confirms the person will proceed towards Enlightenment practicing virtues including discipline, patience and wisdom, but will not enter Nirvana "so long as a single blade of grass remains unenlightened."

Trungpa received lessons in the art of poetry, and in Buddhist metaphysics. In preparation for still deeper spiritual development, his practice included:

• 100,000 full prostrations, each one a move from standing, to lying face-down on the floor, to standing.

• 100,000 recitations of the Triple Refuge — taking refuge in the Buddha, the dharma and the sangha. "Taking refuge" is an oath that commits a person to the Buddhist path.

• 100,000 recitations of the Vajra Sattva mantra.

• 100,000 symbolic offerings.

• 100,000 recitations of the mantra of Guru Yoga, or 'Union with the Teacher.'

At the same time, he was directed to contemplate five subjects:

• The rare privilege given to one to receive spiritual teaching in this life.

• The impermanence of life and everything else.

• The cause and effect of karma.

• The understanding of suffering.

• The necessity for devotion.

***

Trungpa's teenage years were lived in the shadow of political uncertainty. Tibet was completely subjugated by China in 1959, but the invasion took place almost a decade earlier. Chinese troops entered in 1950, quickly establishing a strong presence in

East Tibet and a foothold in the west of the country. When tiny El Salvador called for a United Nations condemnation of the invasion, the matter was deferred. The world's most powerful countries looked the other way.

These years involved more rigorous teachings and new responsibilities for the young tulku. He meditated in caves of holy mountains, sometimes for weeks at a time, and travelled the long distances of his district on foot over snow-covered mountains. He received the degrees of *kyorpon* (equal to a doctorate) and *khenpo* (master of studies). He was enthroned supreme abbot of Surmang, becoming the political overlord of the whole region.

But the outside world was moving in. In 1954 Trungpa saw his first film, a Chinese propaganda piece sent to his monastery in the hope of indoctrinating monks. When asked to become a Communist Party committee member, he politely avoided the commitment. At nineteen Trungpa enjoyed his first ride in a vehicle: a truck. He was so excited that another monk warned him, "You know how strong material forces are: now you are having one of your first direct encounters with them. Study what you are; don't lose yourself; if you simply get excited about the journey, you will never find out what we are really up against."

Tibet in 1959 was up against the world's largest army. At the time the country was isolated, feudal, and spiritual. There was no secular government: the nation was organized along lines prescribed by Tibetan Buddhism. The head of government was the Dalai Lama. The country did not stand a chance.

China has historical explanations for regarding Tibet as a Chinese province — even some leaders of the Chinese democracy movement argue Tibet should not be independent. The Communist government was also incensed that feudalism and religion were flourishing. From a strictly materialistic viewpoint, Tibet was channeling a great deal of resources into keeping the Buddhist religion in a privileged position. Part of this privilege enabled the most educated people in Tibet — senior tulkus — to receive a rigorous and thorough education. Tibet's educated class were learned to an extraordinary degree, and because of this Tibetan Buddhism was remarkably prepared for tragedy. In 1959, when most of the Buddhist leadership, including Trungpa and the Dalai Lama, escaped the Chinese by fleeing to India, they carried the most valuable treasures of their legacy with them — in their minds.

Twenty-year-old Trungpa, using Tibetan methods of divination to help him choose directions, led a group of companions in a winter escape over the Himalayas. They had to walk most of the way and it was brutally cold and arduous. Many people died, and the survivors were reduced to boiling their leather sacks for food.

Trungpa knew they had reached safety when they cleared the mountains and discovered tropical vegetation — a banana tree. Though close to starvation they did not eat the fruit, for fear it was poisonous.

Northeast India was overrun with Tibetan refugees. They joined together to build the infrastructure of a society: hospitals and schools were priorities. The Dalai Lama appointed Trungpa to be spiritual advisor to the Young Lamas Home School, and Trungpa spent the next four years there. Then through contacts in the Tibet Society of the United Kingdom, Trungpa received a Spalding scholarship to attend Oxford University. Just a few years after seeing his first truck, Trungpa was an Oxford scholar.

In class he studied comparative religion and philosophy; day-to-day he took a hard look at Westerners. Most of the Tibetan teachers who had visited the West thought of the "First World" as grossly materialistic and full of barbarians — not a place where the teachings were likely to survive. Unlike the majority, Trungpa actually liked the West. He differed from his fellow monks in another way, too. Most pined to return to Tibet, and hoped it would happen. Trungpa knew the past was the past.

He wanted to teach, and visits to English retreat centres convinced him that a Tibetan Buddhist monastery might be well received in Britain. Trungpa was told of Johnstone House, in the hills of Dumfriesshire, Scotland. He went north to investigate and discovered a small, underused retreat centre. Trungpa proposed a Tibetan Buddhist program, with himself as the primary teacher. After some negotiations, an agreement was made, and Trungpa became the centre's star attraction. He renamed it Samye-Ling, after the first monastery founded by the legendary sage Padmasambhava.

A couple of years later, in 1968, Trungpa was invited to visit the royal family in Bhutan. (The Crown Prince of Bhutan, now King of Bhutan, had been tutored by Trungpa while a student in England.) He included in his trip a ten-day retreat in Taktsang cave, where Padmasambhava had meditated 1,200 years before. Here, Trungpa considered how to best propagate Buddhist teachings in the West. He was deeply troubled. Western students got hung up on the fact he was a monk, and regarded Buddhism as exotic and Oriental rather than accessible to all. He meditated, and considered, and meditated some more. For a few days nothing happened, he wroter later, but then "came a jolting experience of the need to develop more openness and greater energy." In two days he composed a twenty-four-page teaching, the *Sadhana of Mahamudra.*

"Its purpose was to bring together the two great traditions of the vajrayana, as well as to exorcise the materialism which seemed to pervade spiritual disciplines in the modern world... otherwise true spirituality could not develop. I began to realize that I would have to take daring steps in my life."

Trungpa returned to the U.K. For several months he was not sure exactly what action to take. He flirted with leaving monastic life and even proposed to one young woman (now sangha member Maggie Granelli) — who turned him down.

Then one day while driving in Northumberland he failed to turn either left or right, and smashed through the front of a joke shop. Many Shambhala community members believe this is the only time in Trungpa's life in which his mind and body were not in sync, when he was not completely where he was. It was a serious accident: his left side was permanently paralyzed. And he realized that his life had changed — an answer had come, resolving his confusion.

"When plunging completely and genuinely into the teachings, one is not allowed to bring along one's deceptions," Trungpa wrote of the incident. "I realized that I could no longer attempt to preserve any privacy for myself, any special identity or legitimacy. I should not hide behind the robes of a monk, creating an impression of inscrutability, which, for me, turned out to be only an obstacle. With a sense of further involving myself with the sangha, I determined to give up my monastic vows. More than ever I felt myself given over to serving the cause of Buddhism."

Twenty-eight-year-old Trungpa gave up his monk's vows and robes. Shortly afterwards, he married a sixteen-year-old English girl, Diana Pybus. Her family was enraged. So were some members of the London Buddhist Society. Trungpa consulted the *I Ching*, which suggested it was time to cross the great water.

He had been raised in a highly ordered and disciplined society whose roots were ancient and spiritual. As an incarnate holy man his role had been precisely prescribed. Now, suddenly, Trungpa Rinpoche was on his own. Trusting his own teachings and intuition, he exploded onto the spiritual scene in North America — in the midst of cultural and sexual revolutions. He jumped into both, fumbled, fell, and found his own way. Young people, mostly hippies and seekers, came to hear what he had to say. And Trungpa Rinpoche began to teach Tibetan Buddhism — in a way it had never been taught before.

Chapter 3

One Root: Buddhism

The royal household was expecting a birth. King Shuddhodana called his wise men and asked what the future might hold. They said a son would be born, and he would grow to be a great man. But his destiny was unclear. The prince might become a great monarch or, if he renounced his wealth and wandered as a holy man, he would become enlightened.

A baby boy was born, and there was great rejoicing. The child was given the name Siddhartha, meaning "accomplishment of the goal." But the joy did not last. Queen Mahayama, the baby's mother, died seven days after the birth. The king mourned, and he was frightened, too. If the prince grew up and became a wandering holy man, there would be no heir to rule the kingdom. Shuddhodana resolved to ensure that the prince inherit the throne.

Siddhartha was raised in a world most of us dream about. It was luxurious, and seemed perfectly secure. As a boy he enjoyed a life of fun and games, and as a young man was constantly accompanied by beautiful women skilled in the arts of bestowing pleasure.

Of course, the real world has a way of intruding on fantasy. It's true today, in our lives. And it was true in 560 BC, in what is now southern Nepal, for the man who would become the Buddha.

Occasionally Siddhartha would call for a chariot, and go for a ride in the surrounding town. Even then, little was left to chance. Before each journey the king would send staff out along the prescribed route, to clean or remove anything that might be deemed unpleasant.

Thank goodness for incompetent help.

The trouble started when Siddhartha saw an old man, bent over with age. The prince had never seen anything like this before. He asked his charioteer, who explained what aging was and that it was coming for all of us. Siddhartha was so upset he immediately went home. Later trips made him even more uncomfortable. On one he saw a man crippled with disease; on another, a funeral. But on one more excursion he saw a wandering mendicant. The holy man had an upright bearing and emanated serenity. The charioteer explained that such people renounce worldly life and devote themselves to spiritual pursuits.

By this time Siddhartha was twenty-eight years old, married, and the father of a son. And he now realized that the palace life of perks and power, of courtesans and easy delights, was not for him. He decided to renounce worldly pleasures and devote his life to a search for truth. Late one night he took a last look at his sleeping wife and child, and vowed not to return until reaching enlightenment. He slipped out of the palace and was gone.

In nearby woods Siddhartha cut his long, princely hair, and traded his silk clothes for a deer hunter's robe. At first it was rough going. Siddhartha could barely bring himself to eat the coarse scraps of food he begged; sleeping on the ground was uncomfortable. He soon realized he needed a teacher, so walked to a famous hermitage and asked for instruction. He learned to meditate, and was taught the master's metaphysical belief that an eternal principle lies beyond the world of the senses. The former prince was a fast study and soon learned all that was offered. So he went on to another well-known master, and learned yet more levels of meditation. But he knew he was still not fully learned, and left to search some more.

Might asceticism be the path to understanding? The religious world, then as now, had plenty of people claiming that the way to overcome desire is through self-imposed pain and deprivation. Siddhartha decided to try it out, and for six years followed the strictest ascetic practices. Eventually it wore his body down. He became terribly weak, needing help even to wash and to eat the morsels he allowed himself. He was close to death, yet still had not reached the understanding he sought. And he was struck by the realization that to die now would mean his search would end in failure. Siddhartha turned away from the ascetic path and started eating again, a small meal every day.

Shortly afterwards, on his thirty-fifth birthday, the former prince had a long bath in a river, then sat under some trees on the river bank. A young woman came to him, offering a bowl of rice, cream and wild honey. He ate the pudding, and it was good. Then he sat and considered his life and mission. Crossing the river, he accepted a pile of grass from a grass-cutter, and made a cushion under a pipul tree. He swore not to move from his place until he had reached enlightenment, even if it cost him his life.

The night was clear and still. Reaching deeper and deeper levels of meditation Siddhartha found more and more clarity, finally breaking through confusion to see the human condition clearly. He completed his realization just as the first light of dawn appeared. As a testament to his understanding Siddartha leaned forward, and touched the ground.

* * *

Of the thousands of religions in world history, only six have survived, prospered, and now count millions of adherents all over the globe. In order of historical creation they are: Hinduism, Judaism, Buddhism, Christianity, Islam, and the Baha'i faith.

Three of the six — Judaism, Christianity, and Islam — are "people of the book," believing that God's revelations to humankind can largely be found in one holy volume. Hinduism has a full pantheon of manifestations of one great godhead. Baha'is believe that at crucial times in human history God sends a holy messenger, and that Judaism, Christianity, and Islam were established by people of good intentions misunderstanding the message.

Buddhism alone among the six is non-theistic, does not profess a belief in God. Instead of offering up hope for heaven, Buddhists believe heaven and hell exist right here — in your mind. Rather than seek to know God, and so raise our consciousness by experiencing God's presence or following His word, Buddhists work towards clearing up personal spiritual confusion. Doing this, they say, reveals in each of us an innate, awakened state of mind.

Buddhism has a remarkable 2,500 years of evolution, which has produced a variety of schools, hierarchies, and methods of practice. It promotes spirituality, goodness, and compassion. Most of the Buddhists in the Shambhala community, however, are uncomfortable with the word religion. They fear it suggests something formal, dusty, and static, and say Buddhism is none of those things.

"I use the word religion to describe Buddhism only because the world tends to force it on us," says Larry Mermelstein. A Buddhist scholar, he's a member of the sangha team which translates Sanskrit and Tibetan teachings into English. "You could say Buddhism is a way of life, a philisophical system or systems, a way of understanding reality, or a practice to become more clear about the nature of reality. It's all of those things."

Buddhists often refer to themselves as "practitioners" or "students." This recognizes the emphasis placed on practicing meditation and learning from a teacher. Being guided by someone more advanced than yourself is considered an essential part of the process. A Buddhist teacher not only tells students about a text or understanding, but seeks to ignite in each student the power to discover inherent understanding in themselves.

When Trungpa was a boy growing up, one of his teachers told him, "You must not accept anything just because it is given as the teaching of Buddha, but always examine it for yourself. You must follow the Middle Way; if a statement is found in the scriptures, it rests with you to find out what it really means... Each one must follow the guidance of his own inner conscience," Jamgon Kongtrul told Trungpa. "The teacher is within oneself and the way is also there."

This is markedly different from the Christian "I am the way, the truth, and the life." It is, however, in tune with religious and cultural beliefs which place a premium on the personal experience of truth. These would include the gnostic gospels, in which

Jesus says that the two most important commandments are "Do not tell lies" and "Do not do what you hate."

"Interestingly enough," says Richard John, "in Buddhism the very earliest teachings and the very highest teachings are the closest. The whole thing goes like a big O. The practice of meditation and an understanding of basic goodness are basically all that you need. But after you go through all the zillions of Buddhist teachings, and get to the very highest level of Tibetan Buddhist vajrayana teachings, it sounds almost identical. It says, 'Yep, there's nothing else but being in the moment and experiencing your own basic goodness, your own wisdom.' Everything in between is how to do that. Methods and philosophy."

* * *

The Buddha, historians say, is not a myth. He was a real prince, Siddhartha Gautama, of the Shakyamuni clan. He was probably born in what is now the village of Lumbini, Nepal, and became enlightened in Bodhgaya, India. A pipul tree in Bodhgaya has for centuries been honored as a descendant of the tree under which the Buddha (the name means enlightened or awakened one) had his experience of full clarity.

Beyond that, not much is certain. The story of his life and awakening may be apocryphal rather than accurate. It's not even certain what language he spoke.

So much of what we say is in how we say it; great novels and poems are often brutalized in translation. Might not the same thing happen to religious texts? Christianity is often disparaged because no one wrote down the story of Jesus until forty years after his death, but that's practically instantaneous compared to Buddhism. The teachings of the Buddha were not written down for almost eight hundred years.

Muslims have a failsafe system to ensure that the words of the Prophet Mohammed are clearly understood. Arabic was the langugage of the Prophet, and everywhere Islam goes it carries Arabic with it. The Koran is sometimes translated, but it's understood that Arabic is the true language of the Koran. Former pop singer-turned-Muslim Cat Stevens has been out of public view for years, not because he is shuttered away but because he's busy learning the intricacies of a difficult language. This is not so much linguistic imperialism, as an accepting of the fact that some of the nuances and finer points of God's holy word would be lost in translation. God spoke to Mohammed in Arabic — who are people to disagree with His choice? For Muslims one of the proofs that Mohammed was the Prophet is the poetry and prose of the Koran. Mohammed was a merchant, yet he produced the finest writing in the language. Imagine the Bible written by Shakespeare.

Christianity has been less watchful of its words. We know Jesus spoke Aramaic (a language which lives on only in pockets of Syria and, via migration, Sweden), and that the gospels were written in Greek between forty and seventy years after his death. Linguistic scholars and historians now sift back through history, tracing translations, to give us a clear idea of what Jesus said and the context in which he said it.

Buddhism is another story. Unlike Jesus and Mohammed, the Buddha lived in an oral culture. Little was written down; wisdom was passed from teacher to student by spoken teaching. In Buddhism the emphasis is on each student genuinely grasping the teaching, thereby making it their own and waking up to sacred reality. The student can be extremely knowledgable, but if they do not *experience* the truth of the teachings, nothing of value has happened. Words which help you achieve this realization are seen as mere words.

Buddhists believe that reality goes much deeper than language, and language is a poor vehicle to express ultimate truth. But the experience of waking up, of feeling the mind clear, is undeniable. You feel it inside you. Anyone who achieves realization of a teaching can then teach it themselves. In this way each generation passes it on to the next.

Buddhism is, at its roots, a practical philosophy. No particular reading of history is required; no leap of faith is necessary. Its basic tenets are rational and, practitioners say, their truth can be experienced by anyone who spends the energy and time trying.

"It is not a dogmatic faith, in the way religion is usually described," Larry Mermelstein says. "There are many things that Buddhists believe or subscribe to, but the actual notion of subscribing to a belief is fundamentally flawed, because it involves hanging onto a particular view of reality for dear life. All Buddhist teachings and all Buddhist sects agree on this. Nevertheless, one works with one's mind, and one's understanding. How you articulate reality can become more sophisticated, or less. That is why there are different schools of Buddhism. Different Buddhist practitioners, scholars, thinkers, and non-thinkers saw things differently, and explained them in different ways."

Disagreements and disputes are accepted as being in the world of conceptualization: created by thought or language. Meditating, on the other hand, is said to reveal the experience of wisdom beyond conceptuality. Beyond thinking.

"The whole tradition, every last bit of it, subscribes to the notion of true, non-conceptual wisdom," Mermelstein says. "There's never going to be a dogma that is correct, because all dogma is conceptual. So much of Buddhism professes the need to go beyond conceptuality that it eliminates a lot of the power of the literature."

Mermelstein says scholars studying oral societies commonly believe that those societies preserve their great works more accurately than societies where everything is written down. People copying words into books inevitably made mistakes, due to translation problems, illegibility, or simple human error, and these mistakes become part of the dogma. When information is spoken, however, it must be thoroughly understood by both teacher and student, thereby protecting the power of the message.

When the oldest known Buddhist texts in the world, dating to 400 AD, were recently found, he says, not much was discovered. "They didn't provide radically new readings. It did nothing to change anybody's view of anything, which is a good sign that the tradition has been handed on, generation by generation, fairly accurately. Of course it's changing all the time, so the fact that something might have been different long ago is to be expected. There's nothing in Buddhist literature that is so absolute, in the way the Bible is in the Jewish and Christian traditions.

"Undoubtedly in Buddhist history there are teachers who are charlatans. All traditions have these problems. But the Buddhist tradition seems to have some amount of self-correction, in that the people who study the texts develop their intelligence to see through the problems of a faulty teacher. In Buddhism you are always being encouraged to examine something for yourself, to use your own intelligence to evaluate an explanation or teaching. Never are you told, 'You must just believe this.' Never."

* * *

After reaching enlightenment, the Buddha wandered. Near Benares he met a group of ascetics with whom he used to practice; they became the first people to hear of his discovery. He wanted to tell them that yes, people can become fully awake, fully alive, fully aware of the human condition — and be empowered by this understanding. But instead of talking of clarity or enlightenment, the Buddha began with something everyone can relate to: suffering.

There are Four Noble Truths, he said, and the First Noble Truth is the truth of suffering or dissatisfaction. Everything we do involves suffering, dissatisfaction, or pain. Our minds are constantly creating images, thoughts, and desires. Even when we are happy, discursive thoughts appear. "How can I stay this happy? Can I improve on it? Do I deserve this?" We are preoccupied with double-guessing the future and dwelling on the past, and so oftentimes feel dissatisfied. Life is so distracting we forget how to live now.

This can become so uncomfortable that we actually go looking for the reason. What we find, the Buddha said, is that we are constantly struggling, and this persistent struggle makes us miserable. If we calm down enough to take a close look at how we think and act, we discover what's behind this truth. Pulling our strings is ego. The Second Noble Truth is the truth of the origin of suffering.

Here it gets tricky. If we try to improve ourselves, try to rid ourselves of ego, *that* will become one more gigantic struggle. The sane, innate goodness inside us, the Buddha told his companions, comes to the surface only when we are not engaged in struggle. So eventually we discover the Third Noble Truth, the truth of the cessation of suffering. That is, not striving. This, of course, goes against everything we have learned, and almost everything society rewards as behavior. How do we learn to let go? We need to use discipline, and spend time to wear out the ego. We need to walk a spiritual path.

The Fourth Noble Truth is the truth of the path. The path the Buddha prescribed to allow sanity to shine forth is meditation. Only meditation, he taught, can give us the power not to be overwhelmed by the emotional pull of every whim of mind.

The Buddha also told his listeners — who immediately signed on as his students and companions — of the Noble Eightfold Path. The steps are: right understanding, right thought, right speech, right action, right livelihood, right effort, right mindfulness, and right concentration. He also recommended five precepts. They are to refrain from: taking life; taking what is not given; sexual misconduct; false speech; and intoxicants which lead to carelessness.

The Buddha wanted to help people get in touch with reality, and be the best we can be. He explained how we are all under the control of a nasty creation of our own minds — ego. Ego is so phony it even likes to think we are permanent. Is accepting death too much for mere mortals to bear? The Buddha said no. Without an honest awareness of death, he felt, we are doomed to live lives of confusion and misery. It's an unsavory truth, but we are all going to die. Taxes may be avoided, but death is truly democratic. On an intellectual level we know this, but the ego refuses to accept it. Every illness is seen as a betrayal, as something inexplicable and other-worldly. By everyone but the aged and terminally ill, death is treated like a rumour.

This fear of death is caused by thinking of ourselves as permanent. The ego, the Buddha suggested, has all kinds of tricks to prove that we are separate and lasting. One of the most powerful is the way we use speech, our penchant for naming everything. The process of naming, and then believing that a thing is its name, neutralizes phenomena we might otherwise find threatening. At its most developed, ego goes on the offensive and produces ideologies. Whole systems of ideas are used to provide us with identity, rules of conduct, and an explanation of why everything exists.

Ego is terrified of impermanence, and so clings to belief in a self. This creates gnawing insecurity, a desire to clutch at ideology, and further alienation from what is truly real. Dying is real, the Buddha said, and an acceptance of death is needed to live a wide-awake life.

"The Buddha taught that there are three characteristics of existence," Mermelstein says. "Existence is impermanent; all beings are in the process of experiencing pain and discomfort; and there is no substantial reality to your person. There is no thing there that you can say, 'That's me.' Because when you investigate who 'me' is, you see you are composed of lots and lots of different things. Are any of these things myself? Well, go look. The conclusion the Buddha reached is that there is no self."

No substantial reality? A common analogy is that each of us is like a river. You can see a river, but to identify it exactly is impossible — the river is constantly moving and changing. You can never actually say, "The river is *this*." Similarly each of us changes every moment, both physically and mentally.

* * *

"It's a basic human desire to have something or somebody save you, so you won't have to do it yourself," Larry Mermelstein says. "But that's not what the Buddhist tradition is about. If you are looking for a saviour — Buddhism is not going to provide you with one. We're not saying, 'We're going to take care of you.' No one in the Buddhist tradition says that, including the Buddha. The Buddha is not regarded as the saviour — there's no analogy there at all. He's simply an example of somebody who attained enlightenment, and taught the path towards that attainment. That's all.

"In one of the famous dialogues of the Buddha, someone asked him if there was a God. The Buddha did not answer. Later, asked by his attendants why he didn't answer the question, he explained, 'Well, if I told him there was a God he would believe in eternalism, and if I told him there wasn't a God he would become a nihilist. Both of those are extremes, and I teach the middle way.' The whole point is to not be caught up in any kind of extreme. Not to believe that things go on forever and are permanent, safe, and everything will be fine, and not to believe there is no continuity to anything, which is a more nihilstic view and might make a person materialistic."

Buddhism never comes right out and denies the existence of God. Instead it disenfranchises the question, by saying that the existence of God cannot be proven.

"'Atheistic' is a negative way of saying it," Mermelstein says, "because a person described as an atheist is usually someone with some kind of case against God. Trungpa Rinpoche preferred the word 'non-theistic.'"

While God may not exist as an entity separate from people, Buddhists believe everything is sacred and should be revered. It is a philosophy famous for pacificism, including a dictum against hurting any sentient being.

"The Western idea is that reality can be (exactly determined)," says Richard John, who left the U.S. State Department in Washington to move to Halifax in 1987. "You can always find a smaller atomic particle, or go further out into space. It is literally materialism. Not like wanting to have big cars, but in believing there is still going to be a particle there, and that the universe has a size. The Buddhist view is it's a given that the end point of all this material is just space. There's nothing before or after awake space, and compassion is completely inseparable from awake space. That's the most profound Buddhist view.

"In Buddhism there's the absolute view and the relative view. Relative reality is: you have to have a job, you have to die, (you have to live a day-to-day life). The absolute view is that there's nothing before, after, or beyond awake space. The theistic traditions know that, but have to give it a shape. So it's an old guy with a beard, or a goddess, or whatever."

* * *

Siddhartha Gautama never claimed to be more than an ordinary person. He never intended to start a religion, did not think of himself as a "Buddhist." Becoming fully awake, he said, was possible for us all — others had become buddhas before he articulated the experience, and more would follow. He taught this message for decades, and before he died offered last words personalized for everyone: "Work out your own salvation with diligence." Following his death, his students gathered and agreed to continue spreading the teachings.

Millions of people have followed in the Buddha's footsteps. They do not worship Siddhartha Gautama, but are working — practicing — to also become fully present and awake. The philosophy of the reluctant prince spread to become the dominant religion on the world's largest continent, Asia. Because Buddhists have never been big on foreign conquest and proselytizing, its spread outside Asia was remarkably slow. Buddhism reached North America late in the nineteenth century, and is only now becoming a household word. It received a publicity boost in the 1960s from writers including Allen Ginsberg, Jack Kerouac, and Gary Snyder. Celebrity Buddhists today include actors Richard Gere and Elina Lowensohn, and Adam Yauch of the Beastie Boys.

In every new country where Buddhism has taken root, it has undergone a dramatic evolution. It mixes with a new way of thinking, meets new history and customs — and a new variation is born. This changing to suit different cultures is not only expected, but considered inevitable. All of the variations, however, derive from one of three main styles of practice or schools: the hinayana, mahayana, or vajrayana.

Oldest is the hinayana, also called lesser vehicle or southern Buddhism. It stresses a great deal of meditation and working on yourself. Today it is mainly monastic, and is prominent in Sri Lanka and Southeast Asia. The mahayana, greater vehicle or northern school, evolved in reaction to the narrowness of early Buddhism. Its proponents said, "We won't just sit here and better ourselves, we will go out and help people." It is most strongly represented by Zen in Japan, and is also found in Southeast Asia. The vajrayana, or diamond vehicle, is an outcome of the mahayana, and dates from the first century A.D. It travelled north from India to China, and is now associated almost entirely with Tibet.

It was in Tibet that Buddhism reached one of the highest points of its evolution. Mountainous and remote, Tibet created a remarkable religious system and government. In the ninth century Tibetan rulers invited Indian Buddhists in, not to gain spiritual awakening, but because they admired Buddhist cultural sophistication. The practice and the indigenous Bon religion mixed forces, creating what is now known as Tibetan Buddhism. (One Bon influence is the *lhasang*, a smoke purifying ceremony popular with the Shambhala community.) The new philosophy took hold, and was instrumental in transforming Tibet from a war-like society into a nonviolent nation.

For more than a thousand years after its introduction, Buddhism dominated Tibetan life. The power of the monasteries grew to such a point that, in 1642, Tibetan Buddhism acquired dominance in the country's political affairs. After that, Church and State were practically interchangeable terms. The Dalai Lama, the head of the most political Buddhist school, commanded two separate civil services, comprised of 175 specially trained monks and an equal number of hereditary lay nobles. Society was divided into upper and lower classes, clearly defined, and everyone knew their place. No code of laws existed; the country was guided by custom. It was not idyllic. Some of the powerful were corrupt, even when choosing tulkus; the poor were not always treated with respect.

Trungpa Rinpoche was one of the generation of tulkus who saw the world of Tibetan Buddhism crushed. He was nineteen when the Chinese took power in 1959. Monasteries and convents were attacked, and thousands of monks and nuns imprisoned or killed. According to the 1992 National Film Board production *Song of Tibet*, more than a million people have died in the occupation, and Tibet is now the launching site for Chinese nuclear weapons aimed at Europe and the Middle East. Chinese have been encouraged to settle the country, and hundreds of thousands have done so. Columbia University professor Robert Thurman told *Shambhala Sun* magazine that the population of the capital city, Lhasa, ten years ago was 110,000 — 40,000 of whom were Tibetans. Today, there are 400,000 people in Lhasa, of whom only 35,000 are natives.

Tibetan Buddhism has stayed alive by educating new students and tulkus, mostly in India and North America. The Shambhala community founded by Trungpa is one of the largest Buddhist groups on this continent. It is vajrayana, the diamond vehicle.

"A narrower school of Buddhism would be much more Buddhist-looking," says Richard John. "You would think Buddhist thoughts, you would do Buddhist things, and you would be a doctrinal Buddhist. That would be a hinayana thing. The more Buddhism expands, the more that becomes less visible. It becomes a little more open, more unpredictable, expansive, and engaged — to the degree that at the vajrayana level it starts to go to extremes.

"You could go all the way with the yogic thing and become a cave-dwelling yogi, giving up everything, out to penetrate reality as much as you can before you're dead. Or there's what we're doing. Which is, it looks almost normal. It's as normal as possible and still keeping the thread of understanding of the teachings, and the tension and bond with our teacher. So it turns into a sangha, a community."

Chogyam Trungpa's first trip to Nova Scotia culminated in meeting the Apple Blossom queen and her court in Kentville.
Photo: Vajradhatu Archives.

Chogyam Trungpa and friends in the Cape Breton Highlands, 1979. From left: David Bolduc, Judith Smith, Cynde Grieve, Trungpa, Margaret Drescher, Carolyn Gimian and Jim Drescher.
Photo: James Gimian, Vajradhatu Archives.

The Halifax Shambhala Centre and Shambhala International headquarters, 1084 Tower Road. Before 1986, the building was a Knights of Columbus Hall.
Photo: Paul Darrow, The Daily News.

A 1992 board meeting of Shambhala International, in the shrine room of the Halifax Shambhala Centre.
Photo: © Diana Church

The Halifax Shambhala Centre hosts a variety of events. In August 1996, *This Hour has 22 Minutes* star Cathy Jones and artist Paul Hannon exchanged wedding vows.
Photo: © Diana Church

Visting Tibetan monk Jamgon Kongtrul with dorje kasung at the Dorje Denma Ling retreat centre near Tatamagouche, Nova Scotia.
Photo © Marvin Moore

Another Tibetan friend of the Shambhala community, Khyentse Rinpoche, with attendants.
Photo: © Diana Church

Halifax Buddhists bow goodbye to Penor Rinpoche (with hands raised) and attendants, following his 1994 visit to enthrone Sakyong Mipham Rinpoche as leader of the Shambhala community.
Photo: © Marvin Moore.

Chogyam Trungpa (centre) in 1982 near
Pleasant Bay, Cape Breton, the future site of
Gampo Abbey.
Photo: Jaynine Nelson, Vajradhatu Archives.

Chogyam Trungpa, Rinpoche.
Photo: © Marvin Moore.

Chapter 4

Another Root: Shambhala

"Shambhala Training is much more oriented to being helpful, to being of use to the world," says David Burkholder. "Buddhism comes from a monastic tradition, so there's always some kind of flavour of 'You'd be doing this better if you were a monk.' Trungpa Rinpoche came along and said, 'Be awake, all the time.' I think Gurdjieff was the only other person who taught this in the West, saying our usual way of doing things is to put ourselves to sleep. We make sure we have enough habits to cover over every situation, so no situation can hit head on and make us experience the raw, frustrating quality of something we haven't thought about. Both teachers said it would be better to face it — waking up would be worth it.

"The message of the Shambhala teachings is to be awake, in contact with your life full-time. Not looking at life as basically problematic, as something you have to withdraw from as often as you can. We are taking ourselves from a point of fear, where we have a barrier between us and the world, to complete openness to the world, and a willingness to go out with complete confidence."

Burkholder, the director of Shambhala Training in Halifax, says he is proof positive of the program's beneficial effects. "I'm an extremely introverted person and if left by myself I'd never come out of my hole," he says. "This got me much further out than anything else I tried. I thought, 'If it works for me, it will work for other people.'

"I feel good presenting this because I'm not making anyone change. I am offering people a path which is possible, and they will take it step by step and change to the degree they want to. Rather than preach at people, 'Come do it my way and be saved,' which has a lot of levels of manipulation, this says, 'Think of yourself both as basically good, and that you can manifest that.' See what happens when you start to think those ways. Does it mean you make different choices? You'll be able to tell from that if this is something that works for you."

Most people in the Western World do not have the time nor the inclination to study Buddhist teachings. Most of us live fast, busy, complicated lives — and for the most part like it that way. While few people are looking for an eightfold path, almost everyone hopes to understand themselves better, to avoid emotional and mental potholes, and become a better and happier person. To this majority, Trungpa offered Shambhala Training.

Unlike Buddhism, Shambhala Training does not define the many levels of human consciousness. It does not explore the exact shape of reality, the four noble truths and eightfold path. Shambhala Training is founded on the premise that innate human wisdom can help solve problems in the secular world. It aims to ignite a wakefulness similar to that Buddhism offers — but without the philisophical or religious underpinnings.

It's a common theme in popular psychology that every human action is motivated by one of two things: love or fear. Shambhala Training provides a forum where anyone can confront their fear. By facing fear, the theory goes, it is transformed into fearlessness. The resulting shift in attitude makes it possible to relate to the basic goodness in ourselves and the natural world. And this wakes us up to be more genuine, stronger, and compassionate people.

Trungpa used the term "warrior" to describe people who do this, figuring it was the nearest English equivalent to the Tibetan *pawo*, "one who is brave." Shambhala Training is based, in part, on principles of courage embodied in the ancient civilizations of India, Tibet, China, Japan, and Korea. Trungpa prescribed the

Shambhala teachings for people who have lost the principles of sacredness, dignity, and warriorship in their lives.

Up until 1976, Trungpa mentioned Shambhala only rarely. But during a retreat in rural Massachusetts in 1977-78, he began a series of writings on Shambhala and requested aides to initiate a secular, public program of meditation, to which he gave the name Shambhala Training. When Trungpa introduced these to the sangha in 1978, there was a great deal of dissension. The Shambhala teachings were widely seen as watered-down Buddhism, and many dedicated Buddhists were insulted to hear they might learn something from a secular practice. Some people quit.

Trungpa, however, made the Shambhala teachings a priority. In the next several years he gave more than a hundred public talks on the teachings, and Shambhala Training was offered coast-to-coast. The emphasis has deepened. In 1992 Trungpa's eldest son, the present sangha leader, Sakyong Mipham Rinpoche, changed the name of the entire organization from Vajradhatu to Shambhala International. In Halifax, most sangha members study both the Shambhala teachings and Buddhism, while the great majority of newcomers study only the Shambhala teachings. Practitioners say the teachings are profound, empowering — and common-sense.

It's all the more remarkable, then, that the Shambhala teachings come from a most unusual source. It's called *terma* (pronounced tare-ma, rhyming with air-ma). In Tibetan Buddhism a terma text is one hidden for generations or even hundreds of years. Sometimes they are physical scriptures, hidden by the writer. Sometimes they are mind terma, understood to exist on a mind plane. The person who plants a terma text does so knowing it will be revealed to a person, and at a time, when it is most needed.

"Terma is a Tibetan word that literally means treasure," Larry Mermelstein says. "There are various places treasure is buried. Sometimes it is literally a text embedded in the ground. Sometimes it's somehow put inside crystal, sometimes in a rock. Most terma comes from the teacher Padmasambhava. He and some of his disciples composed thousands of texts to benefit people in future ages, and he deposited them in various places. Mind is one place these treasures are placed. They are placed somehow in the thought and intention of realized beings.

"The oldest school in Tibetan Buddhism, the Nyingma, has thousands of such terma traditions. A particular teacher with great realization discovers certain terma, writes them down, and usually develops various practices to make them useful to people. A whole tradition then grows up around those terma. Trungpa Rinpoche is one of those people who discover these treasures. Upon discovering them he was able to write them down, and they form the root texts for the Shambhala tradition."

Mermelstein says that, in conversations with Trungpa, he came to understand that the terma Trungpa received — all in Tibetan — was from Gesar, a mythical figure and king in Tibet. Gesar is regarded as an incarnation of of Padmasambhava, the legendary teacher who more than a thousand years ago helped bring Buddhism to Tibet.

There are references to the Shambhala teachings in many Tibetan Buddhist texts, but no person or source holds absolute authority as to what is or is not recognized as terma. When a teacher proclaims that he has received teachings, and other teachers accept them as genuine, they become part of the canon.

"I'm nervous when people start talking of the teachings as terma," David Burkholder says. "Not that they're not, but to me that leads people into thinking it's weird. It doesn't make them more precious because they came a certain way. To me, these teachings are self-evident when you connect with them. The idea that there could be such a thing as terma is not problematic to me. You find people in Cape Breton who say, 'Ashley MacIsaac has the music in him. That whole family did.' Well, same thing, isn't it? There's a lineage and someone picks up a fiddle and starts to play without being shown. That's what we're talking about. Some kind of transmission of a whole body of something and we don't understand how it happens. You can call it terma or call it something else. What's important is that when you experience it, you know there's a quality there that is so alive, humans could never kill it. What's problematic is calling it something that's not a local expression."

Trungpa first began receiving terma in 1976 or '77. Jan Watson says that his receiving the teachings made for memorable times.

"It was amazing, but he was so uncommon and odd anyway," she says. "Not in a spooky way — I never found him spooky, but not conventional for sure. It was more of this profound, powerful, egoless stuff. It was amazing: 'Oh my God — what is *this*?' It was overwhelming and confusing, because it was so new. We were just getting to understand the Buddhist thing and suddenly we're getting all this other stuff as well. He was very energized by it, of course, because it was very exciting. He would stay up days and nights, stay up three or four days talking and explaining it and then sleep two days solidly."

Watson remembers one event in particular. In November 1978 Trungpa was at the Karme Choling retreat centre in Vermont to present a weekend program. While there, he stayed at a house over a hill from the rest of the buildings. A few people were invited to dinner.

"After dinner he sat down in the living room and started to talk. David Rome, who was his secretary, suddenly realized he had to take notes. And it went on all night. It was cold. It was very cold. Rinpoche had all the windows and a door onto the porch open because he didn't want us to fall asleep. We were all in our nice clothes for dinner and all these windows were open — it was freezing cold in November. Every time he would go to the bathroom or there would be a break, we would say to the people staying in the house, 'Have you got anything I can wear? I'm freezing.' Someone put longjohns on under her skirt. It was just freezing cold, and it went on and on and on, slightly incoherently because we hadn't seen the text at that point, and so this commentary wasn't making any sense to us really. And as soon as we got all the clothes in the house on, he decided we could close the windows. So we fell straight asleep.

"On the way home — at dawn — Karl Springer said to me, 'Have you ever wondered what it would have been like to have been on Vulture Peak Mountain when the Buddha was teaching the Heart Sutra? This is the same.' The Heart Sutra is chanted every morning by Buddhists of most schools in their different languages. It was first taught 2,500 years ago. And here was Karl saying, 'This is it. This is Vulture Peak Mountain, Shambhalian version.' And he said, 'Isn't it a pain in the ass?'"

Watson laughs heartily at this. Having your teacher be insightful is one thing; to be told he is receiving mind transmissions planted by a legendary guru a thousand years ago is something else again. It was outrageous, exhausting, exhilarating, and confusing.

"I was never scared," Watson says. "Maybe I should have been, but I was never scared. Some people were scared. Maybe I was too stupid to be scared."

Why did she believe Trungpa was getting the texts he said he was getting, or that they were coming from the source he claimed?

"To answer that one goes back to the Buddhist-Shambhala teachings," Watson says. "This is a way to live your life so you can become saner and more helpful. The only way to do that is to practice and examine your own experience. 'Don't take anything on faith,' he said frequently. 'You have to test it for yourself, and see if it's true for you.' So one was sort of doing that all the time. As he talked we sort of deceived ourselves that we were understanding it. But later you'd go back and go, 'Oh, oh yes. I see now what that meant.' It was sort of multi-layered stuff. He talked in multi-layers. It says in the Bible that Christ spoke with many tongues; this is the same thing. You hear what you hear, at whatever level you can hear. What you hear and I hear and another person hears is different. I never thought of that quote that way until realizing that Rinpoche was teaching on so many levels."

Considering its remarkable source Shambhala Training is, in a sense, mild stuff. Rather than profess something outrageous, it suggests people can stay sane and be open to one another simply by discovering our own innate goodness. Human nature, according to Trungpa, is basically good — at our core is a soft heart. By getting in touch with innermost goodness, we put ourselves in a position to allow all kinds of positive energy into our lives. The necessary ingredient is courage. It takes courage to live a real life, courage to stay in the moment, courage not to cover our hearts.

"Everyone knows what it is like to feel things directly," Trungpa wrote in *Shambhala: The Sacred Path of the Warrior*. "Intense emotion — passion and aggression and jealousy — don't have a language. They are too intense in the first flash. After that first flash, then you begin to think in your mind: 'I hate you' or 'I love you' or you say, 'Should I love you so much?' A little conversation takes place in your mind.

"Synchronizing mind and body is looking and seeing directly beyond language... You begin to realize that you have a perfect right to be in this universe, to be this way, and you see that there is a basic hospitality that this world provides to you. You have looked and you have seen, and you don't have to apologize for being born on this earth.

"This discovery is the first glimpse of what is called the Great Eastern Sun. When we say sun here, we mean the sun of human dignity, the sun of human power. The Great Eastern Sun is a rising sun rather than a setting sun, so it represents the dawning, or awakening of human dignity — the rising of human warriorship. Synchronizing mind and body brings the dawn of the Great Eastern Sun."

Shambhala Training teaches a way to synchronize mind and body. It isn't easy. As in Buddhism, it's the sitting practice of meditation. Between once and several times a year all Shambhala Centres offer Shambhala Training weekends. Following an introductory talk Friday night, most run Saturday and Sunday from 9 a.m. to 5 p.m. Not including breaks for lunch and tea, ninety per cent of the time finds the students meditating. Once a day a personal interview is held, where instructors ask how it's going and problems and theory are considered. There is a talk and group discussion at the end of each day.

Shambhala Training is organized into various levels. Discussion and reading become more developed in the higher levels, but meditation is the key throughout. Many people take one or two or three levels and do not return. Burkholder estimates 1,200 people have taken Shambhala Training courses in Halifax. Close to half came back for a second weekend. Most of those completed at least five levels.

Weekend levels one through five each have a colorful name: The Art of Being Human; Birth of the Warrior; Warrior in the World; Awakened Heart; and Open Sky. These five are designed to provide anyone with the basic principles of warriorship and the tools to establish a personal meditation discipline. Anyone who wishes to continue on to "graduate" levels is asked to sign on as a sangha member, confirming that they are dedicating themselves to this path.

In the five graduate levels meditation is complemented by talks on spirituality, and spiritual symbols and ceremonies are introduced. Anyone who completes all ten levels is invited to the annual Warrior Assembly, a two-week retreat where the daily schedule includes meditation, study and discussion, formal talks, and social events. Every two years there is also a three-week Shambhala Training seminary, taught in part by the sakyong.

"Shambhala Training teaches people to live in Shambhala," Burkholder says. "It's the common aspiration of humans to have a society that works, that pulls us forward. A society where people could be enlightened rather than know society is structured in opposition to enlightenment. Rather than people constantly feeling 'This society is against me' and 'Do I get value for my taxes?' people would want to pay their taxes, because they see they get value. Our society does a lot of things, but it does them in such a way that people don't even appreciate the things that are quite workable.

"A lot of this is based on exaggerated selfishness, both on the part of individuals and of society, and this creates defensive postures or aggression. When you practice meditation, you realize you do a lot of those things. You might notice that when you're angry you start creating revenge scenarios rather than saying, 'Oh — anger. Lots of energy. I can get my house cleaned this afternoon.' You can turn anger into something useful."

Burkholder was raised a Mennonite, but as a university student in Alberta in the early 1970s embraced hippie culture. "I heard the messages in the music and moved to the country. At that time, very naively, anybody who had done a few psychedelics and been to a rock festival or two thought they had a good idea for a better way of life. So I moved to rural Nova Scotia, to a piece of land and semi-existent house, and retired to the countryside at age twenty-five."

Through the 1970s Burkholder considered his spiritual search to be "self-guided." Then a friend recommended he read Trungpa Rinpoche's *Cutting Through Spiritual Materialism* (Shambhala Publications). He did and immediately felt a connection with Trungpa's "way of explaining what was going on inside of me as I tried to follow some kind of a spiritual path." When sangha members started moving to the province, Burkholder was thrilled.

He recalls Trungpa giving an early talk at the Lord Nelson Hotel in Halifax and being struck by the realization, "He's not talking about Buddhism as it existed in the time of the Buddha. This is live, on the spot. And the teachers who taught me Shambhala Training manifested that quality."

Burkholder, who teaches chemistry labs at Dalhousie University, rereads *Cutting Through Spiritual Materialism* every three years. Not all of it — only as much as he is comfortable working with. The director of Shambhala Training in Halifax read the closing chapters of *Cutting Through* for the first time in 1996.

"This warrior is not aggressive and hard, macho and armoured," he says. "He has a front where the heart is fully exposed, so contact with the world is complete and exquisitely connected. Everything affects you. 'Genuine heart of sadness' was Trungpa Rinpoche's term for this. So rather than something irritating being stimulus to close down, it's stimulus to open further. At this level, humans are very similar. We have all kinds of different thoughts, but the number of our feelings are a small collection, and common. The invitation of warriorship is to open up further. The great thing about Shambhala Training is you get in touch with your basic goodness and so can activate it more. Once you do that you start finding it in other people, bumping into it and sharing it more."

Most of us know Shambhala as the stuff of legends, books, and movies. A renowned Himalayan kingdom, it was peaceful and prosperous, with wise and compassionate rulers and citizens who were learned and kind. Shambhala was free from rampant materialism, revered the arts and artisans, and everyone was treated with respect. Legend says that the people of Shambhala practiced meditation and followed the Buddhist path of loving kindness and concern for all beings.

Did — or does — Shambhala really exist? Many Tibetans believe it is real and still exists hidden in the Himalayas. More think it did exist but has long since vanished. One legend says that the kingdom of Shambhala disappeared many centuries ago. When the entire society became enlightened, the kingdom vanished into a more celestial realm. According to this tale, the kings of Shambhala continue to watch over human affairs and will one day return to save humanity from destruction.

Among Tibetan Buddhist teachers there is another tradition that regards the kingdom of Shambhala not as an external place, but as the ground of wakefulness and sanity that exists as a potential within every human being. Trungpa suggested that, from this point of view, it doesn't matter whether the kingdom of Shambhala is fact or fiction. What's important is appreciating and emulating the ideal of an enlightened society that it represents.

"If we try to solve society's problems without overcoming the confusion and aggression in our own state of mind, then our efforts will only contribute to the basic problems, instead of solving them," Trungpa said. "That is why the individual journey of warriorship must be undertaken before we can address the larger issue of how to help this world. Still, it would be extremely unfortunate if Shambhala vision were taken as purely another attempt to build ourselves up while ignoring our responsiblities to others. The point of warriorship is to become a gentle and tamed human being who can make a genuine contribution to the world. The warrior's journey is based on discovering what is intrinsically good about human existence and how to share that basic nature of goodness with others."

Jan Watson, like many Halifax sangha members, no longer thinks of herself as specifically Buddhist or Shambhalian.

"There's no distinction for me. My personal practices vary between the Buddhist ones and the Shambhalian ones. Sometimes they go through Buddhist phases and sometimes through Shambhalian phases. In fact they balance each other. Trungpa said, 'If you get into a snag or a problem in one practice, you can use the other to get out of it.' It seems that way. Buddhism is much more introverted, and in some ways you can say it's more profound. Maybe the Shambhalian stuff is a little more vast, although they're both profound and vast. The Shambhalian is more worldly, and the Buddhist is more religious — both of those have their pitfalls, obviously. In the sort of society we are living, the two really do balance each other quite well."

Watson believes that the Shambhala teachings are the natural evolution of Trungpa's message. Tibetan Buddhism could not be practiced by most people in the West, and this is a practical alternative. "He talked about them being containers, of one being the container for the other. He said that initially Buddhism was the container for Shambhala, but it would change in the long term. Buddhism gave birth to Shambhala, but in the future..."

The Shambhala teachings attract people who might otherwise never meditate. They stress the value of being engaged with greater society, which some Buddhists might otherwise find easy to ignore. But are they truly ancient wisdom? Who's to say Trungpa didn't simply deduce that Buddhism would not catch on in the West, and so invented the Shambhala teachings?

"Well, great idea," says Larry Mermelstein. "Sounds good to me. Practice the teachings. Do they work? Are they helpful? That's the way we will know: it's the only way we will know. Look at Buddhist teachings — who's to know they are true, too? You can say, 'Well, the Buddha supposedly said, and through one teacher to the next the teachings have continued for 2,500 years, so it's a long tradition,' but it only means anything if it works. Can you wake up as a result of practicing? If it does, it has meaning."

"Trungpa Rinpoche wanted to communicate to this part of the world what the Tibetans know," David Burkholder says. "He did whatever he had to do, and opened himself up. To me, the Shambhala teachings are the fruition of that."

Trungpa Rinpoche himself considered the Shambhala teachings to be both ordinary and magical.

"You might think that something extraordinary will happen to you when you discover magic," he said in *Shambhala: The Sacred Path of the Warrior*. "Something extraordinary does happen. You simply find yourself in the realm of utter reality, complete and thorough reality.

"Your own wisdom as a human being is not separate from the power of things as they are. Therefore there is no fundamental separation or duality between you and your world. When you can experience those two things together, as one, so to speak, then you have access to tremendous vision and power in the world — you find that they are inherently connected to your own vision, your own being. That is discovering magic. We are not talking here about an intellectual revelation; we are speaking of actual experience."

Chapter 5

Grounded: Meditation

You are what you think. Thinking — private, rational intelligence — is set on a pedestal in our society. Actions may prove untrue, lies may be told, but thinking is the genuine article. When we seek truth we put on our thinking caps, because we think they're the best we've got.

Buddhists and Shambhalians agree that thinking is great, a wonderful tool for insight and survival. But they also have a distinct way of thinking about thinking. They believe that the common attitude towards thinking feeds neuroses, makes us feel isolated, stifles our ability to love and be loved, is unnecessary, and can be cured. The antidote they use has been shared by millions of people over thousands of years, does not involve drugs or a belief in a higher power. It's the sitting practice of meditation.

It's a common misconception that the point of meditation is to stop thinking. It's not. Thinking is not only an essential skill, it's the sign of an active mind. Thinking is not the problem; the problem is how we regard our thinking. Most of us are immediately attached to all of our thoughts. If you think, "I want to kill my boss," should you feel evil for having such a terrible thought? Does it indicate that you really want to? Meditation practitioners say it's just a thought; nothing to be attached or committed to.

They believe our very identity has become confused. You are *not* what you think.

***

We all talk about getting our act together, getting back to basics, of the need to relax. What we're really wanting to relax is our minds. Rarely do we allow ourselves to honestly rest and be restored. Even on a break in routine — on vacations or weekends or call-in-sick "health days" — we usually opt to escape. Instead of relaxing the mind we go to a movie, play sports, or have a few drinks with friends. Afterwards we are just as exhausted as before, because we didn't really allow the mind to relax. We just filled it up with other stuff.

Meditation sounds boring — and practitioners admit it often is. They also say it offers relief. Instead of thinking, thinking, thinking, and being attached to every idea — you observe the mind creating thoughts. Thinking, thinking, thinking, the theory goes, doesn't solve problems anyway. It just stirs them around.

Adulthood in some ways consists of undoing the confusions incurred when we were children. No parent can do a perfect job of raising a child. No parent is perfect to begin with and then life gets in the way, mucks things up, confuses the issue. So we all grow up and carry into adulthood deep-seated problems. When we say "getting our act together" we often mean becoming free of these hidden, longstanding confusions. But it's tough sledding, because life gets in the way for us, too. We all have lives to live. So we squeeze into our hectic schedules a few self-help books, an hour a week of therapy, or accept that this is just the way life is, unfortunately.

Meditators say sitting can dissolve some of the muck, leaving you stronger, healthier, and more able to live a fulfilling life. It can have you feeling wide awake. They believe it, they say, because it has happened to them. By taking breaks to relax, the amount of confusion and noise in the mind eases. In place of confusion they experience what had been covered over: inherent goodness.

"Ego is the word for all that stuff that's obstructing basic goodness," says Richard John. "It's not a thing, it's just an accumulation of habits, baggage, and confusion. It's layers and layers of hope and fear and dreams. It's that pile of stuff which obstructs the simplicity of what is already inherently brilliant and happy, clear and compassionate. It's just a word for the junk. Ego has to do with habitual patterns that make you feel separate, make you like and dislike everything according to your little limited view of things. It has to do with accumulated ideas that make you think you are a solid entity with a past and a future. But there really isn't anything there: it's just a whole bundle of all these habits. In meditation you allow the dissolving of all of this baggage. One image that's used is: you don't get rid of ego, you just wear out the habits, like old shoes that fall apart. It's basic Buddhist and Shambhala philosophy that basic goodness is real and ego isn't."

In much of the East, meditation is regarded as a perfectly normal activity. Although practiced by contemplative traditions throughout Western history, including many schools of Christianity and Judaism, in the West today meditation is considered foreign.

"Practicing meditation is discovering our own wealth, our own sanity," says Shambhala community leader Sakyong Mipham Rinpoche. "People feel you need to go into some sort of trance, you need to go somewhere else, you need to escape. The hardest thing to recognize is that it's right here, in our body and mind. When we say we want to go to the beach, we want do this and that, what are we saying? We want to get away from ourselves. We feel the answer has to be somewhere else because 'I've been stuck with myself all this time, and I know it's not here.'

"Meditation is not easy; it's challenging. Because you took so long to create (your habitual way of thinking), it's going to take a little time to unravel it, to work with it. In the West people think of meditation as exotic. But it's traditional, straightforward, and considered the norm in many places. Meditation is not Asian. It is discovering who we are."

Meditation promises no magical solutions, but it can help many people live more fulfilling lives. Does everyone need it?

"Plenty of people have never meditated and have real awareness; other people have been meditating for years and have real problems," Richard John says. He is one of two Haligonians involved in a three-year meditation retreat at Gampo Abbey in Cape Breton. Thirty people began the retreat in 1991. They are doing it in six month stints: six months on, six off. "Everybody has different circumstances they are working with. It's never said anywhere that nobody knows anything until they start doing this. That's not true. There are people who are very awake who have never heard of it. It's a key idea in the Shambhala teachings that wakefulness is a basic human trait. Everything else — how you uncover it, remember it, discover it — is just method."

For those who do learn to meditate, instruction is necessary. The mind can create both heaven and hell, and is a dangerous thing to experiment with. Learning from a seasoned practitioner is recommended. There are dozens of variations in technique, different ways to use the breath or visual reference points. All aim at pulling away the gunk and letting inherent wisdom shine forth. The technique used by Buddhists and Shambhalians in Nova Scotia was devised by Trungpa specifically for students in the West. It is based on the *shamatha* meditation practiced by the Buddha.

"Trungpa Rinpoche tried to find a balance that was most penetrating for Westerners," John says. "In Tibet and Nepal, traditional Buddhist teachers would start you doing all kinds of other practices. Visualizations, prostrations, mantra — all kinds of active, complex practices. Rinpoche said that was because those countries had cultural and religious ground established that we don't have. There was already an orientation toward simplicity, as opposed to our fixation on achievement, activity, and individuality."

Those cultures also had more patience. In the West we want our fixes to be quick and, hopefully, easy. Sitting meditation is not easy, nor is it quick. It may produce some early positive results, but the work of letting go of decades worth of habitual thinking and reaction is just that — work. Meditators tend to talk of the practice joyfully, but they are referring to long-term effects. The actual hours spent sitting, all admit, is at times intensely difficult.

"You're not just recharging your batteries or going off on a thirty-minute mental holiday," John says. "It doesn't make sense to look at this kind of meditation without seeing it as a long-term path. On the other hand, any teacher will tell you, 'If you don't have time to sit more than ten minutes every now and then — that's wonderful, do that.' Still, this is not a quick fix. It's definitely not a quick fix.

"The catch-22 is that if you give up the idea it's going to make you feel good, it probably will. Irony and paradox are a very interesting part of this because you're beginning to undermine the habitual dualistic mind. That's what irony and paradox are all about — you can't quite put it in a box, right? You can't quite make a comfortable duality: this is good, that is bad. You're outsmarting your habits and your whole intellectual stance.

"There's a distinction made in Buddhism between the view and the practice. The view is that if one does the meditation practice all kinds of wonderful things happen. The view is that confusion will subside, your mind will become more clear and precise, sources of pain will lessen. You'll find more appreciation and happiness in more areas, without being so limited in your attachments. You'll find more situations become workable and difficulties become inspiring. Obstacles become just natural occurrences, and not particularly a big deal. Emotional ups and downs become more even."

The view, of course, is relatively easy. The hard part is the practice.

"The idea of meditation is that it's the most direct way to manifest innate intelligence, as opposed to thinking and talking about it," John says. "You're basically working with three things. Your body, your mind, and the energy that goes back and forth between you and the environment — what is traditionally called the speech condition. Your body, mind, and a sense of relationship with other stuff — that encapsulates your whole reality. There isn't anything else.

"It's all about setting up conditions. You are trying to generate the conditions that will allow the direct experience of simplicity and awareness to occur. You're trying to subtly manipulate the body conditions, the mind conditions, and your connection with the world so that natural, simple awareness can rise to the surface.

"The starting point is always body, because it's most basic and obvious. So you start with the body, and the first thing you do is stop moving. You sit. Because you're a human being and intended by design to be upright, uprightness is a crucial part of it. So the posture is very erect. The first part of the posture is solid and grounded, which is the way you put your rear end on the cushion. From there on up, everything is upright. You're not curling up or hiding or avoiding — you're not going into any kind of mental closet. So it feels oddly exposed. Trungpa Rinpoche talked about head and shoulders being upright. It's not a military kind of rigidness — he said it was like the head and shoulders were being pulled from above. Within this directness there's a kind of relaxation.

"The rest is details. The legs are allowed to be comfortable, the arms are allowed to fall to the sides naturally, and the hands are placed on the thighs. The eyes are open. This is partly a practical matter of not getting too introverted and drowsy. It's also a matter of acknowledging that you are relating with things exactly as they are. You're not in a dream world or visualizing a better place. Wherever you are is where you are. The body is grounded, but also very upright. Trungpa said, 'You have a sense of a strong back, and a soft and vulnerable front.'"

The practice of meditation is key to understanding Buddhists and Shambhalians, because it is key to how they understand themselves. Most have small shrine rooms in their homes, and a regular time to practice or "sit." A small shrine is set up, holding incense, photos of teachers, and other aids to focusing thought.

The aim is not to murder the ego. It's a common misconception that meditation is a full-bore assault upon the ego. This usually walks hand-in-hand with another misconception: people who meditate are weak, indecisive, and unfit for life in the modern world.

"When asked about that Rinpoche would always laugh and say, 'Enlightened people can still cash cheques and cross the street. In fact, you can do it better,'" John says. "That's why it's misleading to think of ego as an identity you're getting rid of. Rather than getting rid of something, it's more like clarifying what your true identity is.

"The technique is to use the breath as an anchor for attention. It's the occupation that you give yourself while sitting on the cushion. With virtually nothing to do, you have to do something. The mind has to have some kind of tether, so it's given the breath. This tradition is slightly different from other Buddhist techniques, in that a separation is made on attention on the inbreath and the outbreath. We put the attention on the outbreath and then just drop it during the inbreath. It goes like this: I'm sitting here on the ground, upright, holding a sense of strong back soft front, and my focus is on the breath going out, and then it dissolves. Go out. Dissolves. Go out. Dissolves. It isn't just continuous concentration. The point is to actually break the concentration, rather than let it become solid. You let go of the anchor. You use the anchor, the breath, to take you to no anchor. That's the idea of going out and dissolving. You let your breath gently take your attention outwards and then just leave it. So you're cultivating a kind of direction: going out.

"Not just in the sense of air coming come out of your nose and going in front of you. It starts with that, with something literally coming from inside your body and going outside. But the more a person settles into it, the more the going out part becomes a sense of relaxing outward, of just expanding. So the breath is a reminder you use as a natural, self-existing reference point. It's not static, it moves between this and that, and that's the speech part — how to move between me and my world. My body and the environment — the breath is both. It goes inside and outside.

"While you're resting in this posture, you become aware of the activity of your mind. You're sitting there, nothing is happening, but all sorts of stuff is happening. Memories of the past. Projections into the future. Thinking about the present. Buddhists call it the three times: past, present, and future. Your mind is constantly wandering through this past/present/future permutation. Or a stronger kind of energy comes along, which is what we think of as emotions. So as well as thought, there can be feelings of irritation, or feelings of boredom, or feelings of longing or lust or jealousy. These are not just discursive thoughts — there's more energy. Then there's also external perceptions: the senses. Sounds come into your mind, you see colours and so forth.

"All of that stuff, whether they are what we normally think of as thought or emotion or perception, are all regarded as thought. In meditation practice you are not making any kind of judgment between types of thoughts, emotions, or perceptions. You are only discriminating as to whether there's thought or not. In other words, the mind becomes aware of itself. When awareness notes that it's thinking, it interrupts the thought process. The whole idea is to watch your mind and just be.

"As a kind of trainer wheels approach we label it thinking. So whenever you notice you are thinking, you note it: 'Thinking.' It could be pleasant, it could be awful, but no distinction is made. (Obviously, a distinction is made, because you feel happy, or sad, or nothing.) But the shamatha technique is to rest in your body and just be aware of your thought process. So if you hear a car drive by — thinking. If you have an ache in your knee — thinking. If you have a memory of childhood — thinking. If you suddenly smell lunch cooking and realize you're hungry — thinking. If you suddenly have a great insight about what the whole purpose of meditation is — thinking. That's when it gets really interesting, when you start thinking you're supposed to have spiritual insights and actually you are just supposed to label them thinking."

* * *

"Practicing meditation makes it easier and easier to catch yourself," says Colorado sangha member Alyn Lyon. "To realize, 'Whoops — thinking.' So if you get angry you can say, 'Whoops — thinking,' calm yourself, and then deal with the situation. It doesn't mean the buttons won't get pushed — they will. But you aren't being controlled by every emotion into actions you might later regret. You have discipline and are living with your mind complementing yourself, instead of being just a mind."

Halifax sangha member Crane Stookey says he discovered there is more to meditation than he first thought.

"This technique purports to be working with mind, but is actually working with heart. It's not an intellectual exercise — even for people who go in with an intellectual viewpoint, who think it will make them more efficient, etc. In my first month-long sitting program I felt tremendous sadness and tremendous generosity. There was the experience of tenderness and sadness, of relating to the suffering of the world. It's not about trying to stop thinking. It's more a matter of bringing curiosity and gentleness to your thoughts. If you see the world as a manifestation of energy you can see thoughts as a manifestation of mind — the play of the mind. That's all. They're neither good nor bad."

* * *

"The idea while sitting is not to put as much attention as you can on the breath," Richard John says. "Trungpa always said you actually put only about a quarter of your attention on the breath. You're being pretty lighthanded. You're not trying to squeeze it into a tube, or control it, you just want to anchor your mind enough that you can observe it. So you have a little bit of detachment, and a little bit of anchor, but beyond that you're trying not to interfere with your normal thought process too much.

"Then anything can happen. Anything! Whatever is going to come up, comes up. It might be soothing, contemplative thoughts, or remembering something painful that's been bothering you for weeks. You attempt to regard all these things through the same lens, without getting lulled by the pleasant stuff or freaked by the unpleasant. There's a kind of agreeing to be put in this container and allowing whatever is going to happen to happen, with no attempt to feel better afterwards. You might feel worse afterwards. You could feel anything. This attitude is usually called making friends with yourself. It's like, if you're being introduced to a person, you don't immediately start planning that they're going to be a certain way. If you're going to be a friend you just see how they are, and try to relate to them. As opposed to saying, 'I'm going to improve you.' So it's not an attitude of self-improvement; it's an attitude of somewhat detached self-acceptance. You're just being present."

The more time we spend meditating, John says, the more we grow accustomed to being in the present, instead of awash in a jumbled mix of past/present/future. So we become more engaged with life, more aware of our options and open to beauty. We develop honesty with ourselves, and begin to realize our power. Naturally, it can be hellish.

"Anyone who practices meditation will see, instantly, how confused they are, how swirling the thoughts can be," Larry Mermelstein says. "Hopefully that humbles you a little bit to know that this is not a simple path of, 'Just do some funny little thing and everything's going to be just great, and let's go out into the world and tell everybody about it.' It's so clearly not motivating a person to do that. Usually we encounter a disturbing amount of discursive thought and habitual patterning. You start to say, 'Gee, if that's what I'm about, what kind of confusion am I creating in the world?' Meditation practice fairly quickly stops a person from polluting the rest of the world, from creating confusion. And you have to start with that before you can ever do benefit."

This suggestion, that one has to get one's own act together before helping others, is not commonly held in society. Mother Teresa is widely praised as a modern-day saint, and most people couldn't care less why she is doing what she's doing. The fact of working with Calcutta's poor is enough, is considered proof of saintliness. Sangha members look at this another way, say that sanity and clarity are the only things that can make *lasting* change in the world. Before helping others, therefore, cleaning up our own act is imperative.

This leads to a common criticism, that Buddhists and Shambhalians spend all of their time working on themselves, and little on charitable works. Richard John agrees that the community has yet to act out its compassion. "We have a lot to learn," he says. "I think that's the biggest theme now starting to emerge in the sangha...

"In the lower schools of Buddhism there is the idea of cessation, where you just evaporate. That's a primitive hinayana view which is denounced by everybody else — it's like getting stuck in kindergarten. The mahayana attitude is that any desire to lessen your own confusion has to be done for the benefit of others. By making a vow to that effect (the bodhisattva vow), it keeps the whole thing vibrant and real, instead of going into a mental cave. The mahayana and vajrayana model of an enlightened person is a very active person engaged with the world."

People who learn Trungpa's meditation technique in a Shambhala centre usually find that their practice evolves from a personal focus to looking outwards. This is part of the design: first to become mindful, and then aware. The shamatha practice evolves into *vipassana* — the second kind of meditation practiced by the historical Buddha.

"The reason you are resting in shamatha is to also have an expanding awareness," John says. "Vipassana is a qualitative awareness that comes along. Shamatha tries to develop stillness;

vipassana is about keeping the same awareness that's present in stillness, even when thoughts are arising.

"Everything about this meditation technique is bringing together a balance of energies. Mind and body. A strong back and a soft front. The precision of seeing the thought and the openness of letting go of the thinking. It's all about subverting the arch-habit: cutting up everything into dualities."

"A lot of activity is needed to slow down and change reference points," says Richard Haspray, who has taught meditation practice at the Halifax Shambhala Centre. "There's a lot of activity involved in learning to rest. The naturalness is self-existing, but we're not all that familiar with it. It's covered over. It's apparent when you discover it, but the process of rediscovering it — is a process. So there is talk about a path. At the beginning one needs to work on your own specific physical, emotional, and psychological situation. It's very individual. When you calm down, you will wake up more to what's going on around you.

"When Chogyam Trungpa, Rinpoche was alive, what people actually shared was the same teacher. He appealed to an infinite variety of people and personalities. Now he's dead. What remains is the teachings, and a whole community of people have connected with these teachings. Now the common element is meditation practice. There's a kind of calmness and peace, a steadiness, and a knowing quality that goes with this.

"The experience is non-conceptual, so you won't understand it until you do it. The idea isn't the experience. You need to do it in order to find out what it is."

* * *

So I did. On weekends in March and July 1996, I signed up for Shambhala Training levels I and II. Four full days were spent sitting in silence. They were often boring, sometimes painful, and occasionally exhilarating. There were two great surprises. One was this: there is nothing exotic or other-worldly about basic meditation. It is not at all a religious practice. All you do is sit there, breathing, and focusing the mind so body and mind can be together for awhile. It's a basic human activity, like sleeping, laughing, or making love. That's all. Yet like those activities, it has the power to resonate through your life.

Which leads us to the other surprise: sitting really does create space in the mind. After two days of sitting from 9 a.m.-5 p.m., I did feel more power to straighten out my priorities, make the right decisions, and live a better life. The word empowered comes to mind. And it didn't feel at all bizarre or otherworldly: it was like an oxygen-blast of basic sanity. Which only makes sense, I suppose. Imagine dedicating two whole days to truly relaxing, to calming your mind down from its regular jumpy busy-ness. That's what it was.

Meditation is a poor name for it, much too passive. You may be only sitting, but it can be an intensely active time. Thoughts come fast and furious. On my first morning I revisited every girl I had ever kissed, won the World Cup of soccer, and died — all before tea break. Since that morning I have sat an average of five to ten times a month, for twenty or thirty minutes each time. This can be frustrating — putting twenty-minute snippets into this probably makes as much sense as learning to play a musical instrument in lessons of twenty minutes. Yet it's all the time I choose to afford.

Practitioners who stay with it say the long-term effects of sitting regularly can be profound. Richard John says there's an extraordinary parallel between meditation practice and the dying process. In both, letting go is not just a metaphor, it's actual experience.

"Doing a meditation practice is a way to let go, whether it's letting go of solid ideas of something, your neuroses, or constant silent talking to yourself. It seems harmless enough, but it's an insidious process. What you are doing is reversing the whole momentum of me me me my life my life my life. It's hard to relate to the idea of letting go of your thought process. It's a subtle thing, and tricky. Every time you cut your thoughts to come back to your breath there's a little dissolving of something. There's a little death. And the further you go with that process the more you start to experience, mentally and physically, what happens when you die.

"Lots of Buddhist books describe the death process, and they always describe this physical process. They call it the elements dissolving. First the earth element dissolves. Your body gets very heavy and weak and you feel like you're sinking and you start to panic because you feel you're losing ground. Then the water element dissolves. That's when everything starts to dry up. Then the fire element dissolves. Your body starts to get cold and you can't move anymore. You see this when people die — it's very literal and visible. These things are also accompanied by mental experiences, certain kinds of sensations. And it's the same ones that people experience when they go into deeper meditation practices.

"You discover two things meditating," John says. "One is it helps your life. But it also gives you a window beyond just making your life work. It gives you the feeling that if you really let go, what's out there is actually okay. Once you get through fear, what's there is really good."

Everyone who has meditated tells strange stories about the experience: tales from the cushion. Some people have to rely on old stories, though, because they have no new ones to tell. Meditation may be at the heart of the sangha experience, but at any given time some people hardly practice at all. Everyone talks about practicing, it's the one experience everyone shares, but not everyone quite gets around to plunking down and doing it. Most sangha members go through phases of enjoyment and progress and times of restless, itchy frustration. The pivotal problem with meditating — boredom — is a frequent topic of discussion.

Richard Haspray has been meditating for thirty years. He has praised its merits to hundreds of people. But like almost everyone, there have been breaks in his practice.

"Sometimes practice becomes stale," he says. "You get stuck behind a veil, in blind alleys. Practice becomes a pattern. There are all kinds of rationalizations for stopping practicing. Part of the problem is the very logic of it: why do you have to practice if you're already enlightened? For me that's been a big one. A lot of times I've stopped practicing just to test it out.

"But I didn't find that I was all that happy. A lot of other problems would arise. You just regress. The same kind of problems that brought you to the path in the first place would reappear. You cover things up by trying to think your way out of problems."

Chapter 6

Wild and Crazy Wisdom

Shambhala community members who met Trungpa Rinpoche in the early 1970s have by now spent months, if not years, sitting on cushions, painstakingly separating the wheat from the chaff of their minds. They are working to become stronger, more compassionate people. You would figure, then, that the man who inspired thousands of untamed spirits to alter their lives so dramatically must be a saint, right? Yet by conventional moral standards Trungpa sometimes falls short of basic decency. He drank to stupefaction, had a hearty sexual appetite, and could be downright tempestuous. He asked his students to "Do what I say, not what I do."

Still, everywhere he went Trungpa attracted people wishing to study under his guidance. The attraction went deeper than charm, was subtler than suavity. It was more profound and complex than sheer force of personality. Many intelligent, skeptical people found in Trungpa a degree of sanity they had never experienced before.

"He was the most intelligent person people had met," says Jan Watson. "It didn't seem to matter what question got thrown at him; it came back as something amazingly intelligent. He was presenting ideas that people had never thought of before. So we were very intrigued and drawn to him."

"A lot of Buddhist teachers who come here talk straight from the text," Jill Scott says. "It's very academic: they have studied the text and they are teaching you what it says. Trungpa

Rinpoche didn't do that. His way of communicating traditional teachings was purely from an experiential point of view. He was able to tune into the audience he was talking to. Young Westerners, in the late '60s. He understood us enough to speak to our experience, to where we were at, what we were looking for, and what we were rebelling against."

"Trungpa was the kindest person I ever met, and also the most terrifying," says Dan Hessey. "There was something about Trungpa — in his presence you were stripped naked. You were completely facing who you are. It was very intense. He was so real that it was almost like you couldn't be in his presence without facing that yourself. He made you realize you wanted to be the best you could be. Once you opened up to that, it was hard to turn away. And you knew he was the teacher who could help you get there."

* * *

"Whatever you do always manifests how you are feeling about yourself and your environment," Trungpa Rinpoche said. "That can always be detected by your gait and your gestures — always. It is as if you were married to your phenomenal world. All the little details — the way you turn on the tap before you take a shower, the way you brush your teeth — reflect your connection or disconnection to the world."

Trungpa, a Tibetan teacher, revealing the nature of physical reality to students born in a materialistic society. Like so much of what he taught, there is irony here. There is also, according to his students, self-evident truth. Trungpa was no ordinary teacher; his teaching style included a share of revelation. He spoke with insight and certainty, but often a person listening — or reading his books — would not immediately grasp the full significance of his message. Later, however, the truth becomes obvious. It is almost as if what he has to say is so unexpected, it needs time to ripen in the mind.

"We have the expectation that spirituality will bring us happiness and comfort, wisdom and salvation," he said at an early lecture. "This literal, egocentric way of regarding spirituality must be turned completely upside down... It is necessary first to see the motivation for our spiritual search. Ambition is unnecessary if we are going to start our path open-mindedly, with a mind that transcends both 'good' and 'bad.'"

Trungpa gave hundreds of lectures and seminars all over the U.S. in the early 1970s, and made forays into Europe and Canada. It was mostly straight Buddhist teachings: the Four Noble Truths, the dangers of attachment, how to meditate. Whatever the subject, whether interpreting ancient texts or the Don Juan books of Carlos Castenada, Trungpa kept the message keenly relevant to the lives of his audience.

One of his favourite themes was spiritual materialism. Over and over he stated the fact: the spiritual path needs a delicate touch, and what some people mistake for spirituality is actually out-of-control ego. He poked holes in the two traps well-meaning Westerners are common prey to: the cultural habit of looking for quick spiritual gratification, and excessive fascination with Eastern traditions.

"There are numerous sidetracks which lead to a distorted, ego-centred version of spirituality," Trungpa said, in a lecture published in *Spiritual Materialism* (Shambhala Publications). "We can deceive ourselves into thinking we are developing spiritually when instead we are strengthening our egocentricity through spiritual techniques. This fundamental distortion may be referred to as spiritual materialism... The basic problems of spiritual materialism are common to all spiritual disciplines. The Buddhist approach begins with our confusion and suffering and works toward the unraveling of their origin. The theistic approach begins with the richness of God and works toward raising consciousness so as to experience God's presence. But since the obstacles to relating with God are our confusions and negativities, the theistic approach must also deal with them. Spiritual pride, for example, is as much a problem in theistic disciplines as in Buddhism."

He taught that critical scrutiny and an eye to self-deception could keep one on an honest path, guiding oneself to recognize and honour innate wisdom. Trungpa was renowned for his ability to see through the most carefully constructed mask to a person's true self. He confronted his students with this discrepancy, in whatever way he thought appropriate, to try to wake them up to being honest with themselves. But while Trungpa was telling students they had the answers inside them, he also suggested they needed help to find them. It's one of the ironies of Buddhism that, while directing everyone to find the truth inside themselves, at some levels it also commands devotion to a teacher.

"It's a Buddhist principle," Jan Watson says. "You have to find a good teacher if you're going to follow Buddhism. Rinpoche talked about that a lot in the early days, and always said, 'You must choose your teacher yourself. You can't just follow someone else's opinion, you have to test it out for yourself.' He was always saying, 'Don't just do what I say; figure it out for yourself.'"

The kind of teaching Trungpa did was highly personal. To gain ground students had to reveal themselves to the teacher. And vice versa.

"Do you know about the teacher, the spiritual friend and the guru?" Watson asks. "In hinayana Buddhism the person who teaches you is your teacher. He teaches you the facts and figures, just like a teacher. In the mahayana the teacher is what they call a spiritual friend. He is your eye-to-eye-level friend, but on a more spiritual level. He is willing to take on your garbage and work with that with you. This is by mutual consent — nobody's doing anything that they're not themselves inviting.

"Then, on the level of the vajrayana, the teacher is the guru, to which you pay homage and devotion. Because the teacher is working with your energy beyond the level of concept and consciousness and feeling.

"For some people Rinpoche was just a teacher — they learned some stuff from him and they moved somewhere else. To some people he was a spiritual friend — he was helpful, they learned and developed and then moved on. And to some people, he is their guru."

Hinayana practice involves meditating and learning compassion. It's calming down to recognize the goodness in oneself, and realizing that this goodness is shared with all sentient beings. On the mahayana level the student comes to accept that fixing up oneself is not enough, and returns to help others in the world. You have to go deeper into yourself, learn humility and the service of others.

Then comes vajrayana. It is even more difficult, because at its highest points the student aims to leave all points of reference — including good and bad — behind. It is an intense practice of working on oneself, especially the worst of oneself. Parts of vajrayana are secret teaching. Without training in meditation, and a clear motivation to help other people, it can be dangerous. Students must take prerequisite disciplines to ready themselves, and be mentally prepared to go through heaven and hell. In order to move completely beyond the hold of the ego, the student submits completely to the teacher. It's a relationship based on no-holds-barred trust.

In vajrayana the teacher is seen as the living embodiment of the Buddha. The student can study the example of someone who, though also human, has developed beyond what the student believes possible. The teacher wants to reveal and work with the student's absolutely naked awareness, and so cuts through the various masks the student might (even unconsciously) wear. Sometimes a vajrayana teacher can be ruthless in tearing away a student's armour, creating pain and suffering. Some students can't take it.

"He worked with people in the way they needed to be worked with," Jan Watson says. "Sometimes to other people that would look nasty. Sometimes people would get hurt, because they were clinging to something he was trying to cut through. When he was trying to pierce an habitual pattern or conceptual mindset of some sort, it needed to be done. And they were asking for it because they were there."

Trungpa taught his students in their language. He was the first Tibetan teacher to teach in English, without a translator. His speaking style was curious: quaint and soft, with a refined English accent. He enjoyed a majestic command of the English language. Trungpa also spoke in a language deeper than regional idiom: he could articulate the language of inner experience. To reach many spiritual searchers in the early 1970s, this was crucial.

"LSD was a big deal then, with students and others," one sangha member said. "It was widely available, and lots of people were doing it. It was opening people's minds in a way they weren't open before. The language of American English could not explain what people saw on acid, and it couldn't explain other insights that people in the counterculture were experiencing at the time. So when people came down, came back from these remarkable experiences, they couldn't talk about what they had experienced. This led to all kinds of confusion and misunderstanding.

"But Buddhism provided that language. It explains so many realms of consciousness, so many ways of thinking. It also provides outrageous imagery: gods representing emotions, that kind of thing. Acid is not like other highs. After coming down you may not be able to articulate it, but inside you know it was perfectly rational, there are steps that were taken, etc. Buddhism is like that as well. There are always steps to explain where you have been, how the mind is working. And like acid it has to be experienced to be fully understood."

"He was able to fully be himself, in a way that made you feel you could be fully yourself," Jill Scott says. "He was just honestly, fully, who he was. He had a tremendous openness and curiosity, never passed a moment by, not even a haircut. He had a lot of energy, and it was as if everything was equally interesting to him. It wasn't like, 'This is a boring thing to do and that is a fun thing to do.' He would welcome any experience — as opposed to most of us, who will pick and choose."

Trungpa's genuineness, his propensity to be fully in the moment, are legendary. And part of that legend is the belief that Trungpa did not think in dualities: good and bad; ugly and beautiful. His students believe he had left all conventional reference points behind. This didn't mean he could not discriminate between what he wanted and did not want. On the contrary, it allowed him clarity of mind to pursue his goals. But no matter what he was doing, he was fully engaged.

"He drank and smoked and had a lot of girlfriends," Jan Watson says. "But nothing was hidden. It was known he had a lot of girlfriends; it was known that he drank and smoked. He wasn't pretending otherwise, whereas some religious teachers were. So it wasn't cloak-and-daggerish. He was very straightforward. People came and they went. A lot of people didn't stay because it was weird for them or they thought he was an egomaniac. But nobody was coerced into doing anything."

Trungpa's aim was to train people to be awake to the nature of the mind and the physical world, not to adhere to a particular set of moral guidelines. Compassion and morality do play a big part in Buddhism — if people are awake they are likely to be more compassionate, and the eightfold path and five precepts are a strong moral recipe. Yet Trungpa played by another set of rules. He was wholly unpredictable. On a deep level Trungpa was intensely childlike — an uncommon trait for a grown man. Imagine being led by an intelligent, courageous, five-year-old. Anything could happen.

In Boulder in 1981, thinking an attendant to be less than mindful, Trungpa purposely fell down the stairs. After the attendant, Joshua Zim, helped him up and promised never again to be so inattentive, Trungpa threw himself down the stairs a second time, requiring a trip to the hospital.

On Risser's Beach, just south of Lunenburg, Nova Scotia, Trungpa in 1984 ordered his driver, Suzanne Duquette, to drive down the beach and into the water. She did. The Mercedes ground to a watery halt and needed to be towed out.

On many occasions Trungpa would tell staff white lies. For example, he once told the directors of both Karme Choling and Boulder that each was talking badly of the other. When the directors next got together they immediately started bickering and Trungpa sat back and laughed and laughed. The message was: don't rely on what anyone says. Trust yourself.

"One time he said, 'I'll do anything to wake people up,'" Jan Watson says. "And he did do some pretty weird things. So he could be scary. It could be painful. But we who were his students would go back for more. We would get caught up short because of something that happened but even years later you'd go, 'Oh, I see.' He never did gimmicky things to attract large numbers of people, he was much more genuine than that. He wanted to plant Buddhism to help people. Genuine Buddhism."

His methods, while inside the spectrum of Buddhist experience, were on the fringe. The Kagyu and Nyinmga schools of Tibetan Buddhism — Trungpa's lineage was the Kagyu, but he was empowered to teach the Nyingma — both have "crazy wisdom" lineages. These feature teachers who are outrageously non-monastic and famous for bizarre behaviour. The belief that any activity can be an expression of basic goodness, if conducted with an honest heart and without grasping for permanence, reaches its extreme position in crazy wisdom teachers.

Most of his former students now agree that Trungpa was probably an alcoholic, but at the time his drinking was accepted as part of, even as fuel for, his magic. Trungpa explained that his circumstances were extraordinary, and that for him alcohol was medicine rather than poison. He sometimes gave senior students drinking lessons, instructing them to be mindful of the changes they felt as they drank more. Trungpa referred to his style of imbibing as "conscious drinking," and in an article entitled *Alcohol as Medicine or Poison* wrote, "Whether alcohol is to be a poison or a medicine depends on one's awareness while drinking. Conscious drinking — remaining aware of one's state of mind — transmutes the effect of alcohol... Alcohol's creativity begins when there is a sense of dancing with its effects — when one takes the effects of drink with a sense of humour. For the conscious drinker... the virtue of alcohol is that it brings one down to ordinary reality, so that one does not dissolve into meditation on non-duality." Trungpa was saying that because he had Vajra nature — a mystically transformed physiology — he had to drink in order to ground himself in "normal" reality.

In the early 1970s, however, his wild ways were part of the attraction. Many early sangha members say Trungpa's lifestyle made them feel comfortable with exploring the Buddhist path. Not just comfortable, but permitted. More than one put it this way: "If he had been wearing robes, it would have felt like a holier-than-thou sort of thing." Another said: "Drinking with him, and then discovering the incredible extent of his discipline and practice, convinced me Buddhism was not just for people sitting on mountain tops." Conventional mores including sexual abstinence, teetotalling, and church attendance were not popular with spiritually hungry, twenty-something seekers in the 1970s.

The most famous episode of Trungpa's bizarre behaviour was on Halloween night, 1975. At a party, a very drunk Trungpa ordered a number of sangha members to strip. When two guests, the poet W.S. Merwin and Dana Naone, refused, they were forcibly stripped by guards following Trungpa's orders. The scene was horribly confrontational, and left some students badly shaken. The day after the party, Merwin and Naone met with Trungpa, and agreed to attend his lectures for another two weeks. They did not make public statements condemning his behavior but word spread, and the incident hurt Trungpa's reputation in Buddhist and literary circles. It's also believed to have cost the Naropa Institute's writing arm, the Jack Kerouac School of Disembodied Poetics, two grants from the U.S. National Endowment for the Arts.

Outside of the occasional scare which could have students questioning their own and their teacher's sanity, most sangha members considered themselves fortunate. They felt they were making progress in the battle to know themselves, and that their way of life combined the best of the Orient and the West. Summer seminary in the Rocky Mountains was an especially favourite time. Days of deep, eastern wisdom were followed by nights of spectacular parties. Living was isolated but communal, religious yet secular. Few realized that Trungpa was not out to establish a community of meditative party animals. He saw the parties, the drinking, as steps in a transformation, a phase on the way to a better place. He started making the point strongly in the fall of 1974.

That's when the Karmapa visited North America for the first time. Rangjung Rigpe Dorje, His Holiness the Sixteenth Karmapa, was head of the Karma Kagyu order of Tibetan Buddhism. Trungpa scrambled to make his troops presentable. He insisted on haircuts, on suits and ties and dresses, created a cadre of uniformed bodyguards, and insisted that the Karmapa be treated with the utmost respect and dignity. The Karmapa in turn held ceremonies proclaiming Trungpa Possessor of the Ultimate Lineage Victory Banner of the Practice Lineage Teachings of the Karma Kagyu. For the first time since his arrival in North America, the cool, hippie teacher was seen in the full, ancient light of the East.

After the Karmapa went home, Trungpa began to incorporate royal trappings into the sangha. His home was referred to as the "court," and his wife called Lady Diana. Some students were dismayed by all of these changes. Still today, in a canyon near the Rocky Mountain Shambhala Centre, lives a former student who looks much the way he did twenty years ago, complete with overalls and beard. He is staying true to the rebellious faith of the 1960s, something Trungpa left behind in 1974.

The majority of students, however, having seen Trungpa's wisdom work so often, listened to what he had to say. Trungpa said the unkempt hair, the partying, the counter-culture stance was a disguise or, worse, a shield they were hiding behind. In fact, he told them, there was no shield — and to pretend there was created confusion and wasted energy. Reality, he said, is a kitchen sink reality, and the object is to feel the joy of being fully alive and awake even while doing the dishes.

Dresses and suits were worn. Students began to read and meditate more. The sangha's early excitement, the glow of youthful exuberance, began to fade. This, too, Trungpa said, was normal and to be expected — truth is not so shallow as to be impressed by age or familiarity.

But the revolution was not yet complete: more shocks were coming. In 1977 Trungpa visited Nova Scotia and chose the province as the sangha's home. The next year he introduced the Shambhala teachings. Suddenly he was telling everyone that Buddhism was not necessarily what they wanted or what was best to practice. He started talking about warriorship and how this can be applied to all areas of your life. Some of the Buddhists felt betrayed at this promotion of "watered-down Buddhism."

The great majority of the community shuddered through yet another change of self-image. In just a few years, the original group of long-haired, counter-culture seekers had undergone an incredible transformation. Instead of indulging in every exotic flavor they could find, by 1978 they were wearing dresses and suits, gravitating to jobs, discovering the path of home ownership and worrying how best to raise kids.

Trungpa continued to build the infrastructure of his organization. Still deeply involved in all aspects, he began to delegate more and more responsibilities. He even appointed his eventual successor, giving Osel Tendzin the title of Vajra Regent. But Trungpa wasn't out of surprises. Shortly after moving to Nova Scotia, he pulled the biggest shocker of all. He died.

* * *

Trungpa, his wife, and four children moved to Halifax in early September 1986. Just three weeks later Trungpa entered the Halifax Infirmary with respiratory distress. On September 28 he suffered a heart attack. He was in a semi-coma for seven months, and died on April 4, 1987.

"It's almost as if he lingered there while everybody picked up their own responsibilities," Allen Ginsberg told Barry Miles in *Ginsberg* (Simon and Schuster). "He empowered everybody in that sense, very directly said, 'You've got to do it now.' So when he died, everybody began appreciating how good a job he did despite all the drunkenness."

The official word is that Trungpa died, at age forty-seven, of kidney failure. It has been reported however, that his death had symptoms of cirrhosis of the liver: he was incontinent, suffering from gastritis, and his belly was swollen. Those of us who were not Trungpa's students tend to focus on his alcoholism and messy death, as if those "facts" infer something about his quality as a man. To his students, the messy "facts" of his death reveal only a small and unimportant part of the story. They focus not on how alcohol helped break down Trungpa's body, but on the constant brillance of his mind. Sangha members do not judge Trungpa by normal standards, because they do not believe he was an ordinary person. They honestly see even his drinking as a teaching. For the rest of us, that takes a leap of faith. For those of us who were not his students, it might be impossible to understand.

According to custom, his body was embalmed in salt and arranged sitting upright in the meditation position inside a wooden box. Halifax sangha members sat with the body all night in the Tower Road Shambhala Centre. Outside, foghorns moaned.

The cremation was held at Karme Choling in Vermont, Trungpa's first practice centre in North America. Fifty Tibetan lamas came for the ceremony; the total crowd topped two thousand. As flames engulfed the body, funeral music was played on ancient Tibetan instruments.

Trungpa had composed this message to be read at his death:

"Birth and death are expressions of life. I have fulfilled my work and conducted my duties as much as the situation allowed, and now I have passed away quite happily. It might cause you grief, sadness; nonetheless you should carry on with what I have created and continue my vision. On the whole, discipline and practice are essential, whether I am there or not. Whether you are young or old, you should learn the lesson of impermanence from my death.

"The children should be raised in pure Buddhist fashion. Their upbringing is very important. Therefore both the schools and the home upbringing of the growing sangha members should be taken care of by the parents, or friends, for that matter. The sangha members should not quarrel or create any friction. They should regard themselves as brothers and sisters.

"On the whole, the expansion of Vajradhatu should be one of the most important focuses. My death should not prevent or slow down any vision.

"Born a monk,
Died a king —
Such thunderstorm does not stop.
We will be haunting you, along with the dralas,*
Jolly good luck!"

---

* Dralas is a Tibetan term representing the innate wisdom of the universe. Human wisdom can be a part of this self-existing wisdom and power.

Chapter 7

Rumours and Truth

Nearly twenty years after their arrival, rumours still swirl around the Shambhala community in Nova Scotia. Time and good deeds have tempered speculation somewhat; still, suspicions persist. Tales are told and retold and often believed.

Rarely is it suggested that the Buddhists or Shambhalians are brainwashing innocent people for nefarious ends. Rarely, too, is the damning word "cult" tossed into conversation. Interestingly, the most persistent rumours do not profess immediate concern for longtime Nova Scotians. Instead, they condemn lifestyle and secrecy.

The three most hardened rumours are these: everyone in the sangha is filthy rich; everyone is sexually promiscuous; and the community is readying for battle, with members receiving weapons training in hill camps across the continent. As is often the case with rumours, there's a germ of truth in each of these suspicions.

* * *

Money

Rich. Wealthy. Fabulously well-to-do. The first thing every Nova Scotian hears about the Shambhala community is that they are rolling in dough. "I know people in Nova Scotia think 'the Buddhists' are really wealthy," Andy Karr says. "A lot of people moved to Halifax in a short period of time and bought houses, forcing up the housing market. So we got a reputation as big spenders."

Halifax realtors had never seen anything quite like the boom of 1987-89. Several hundred people suddenly appeared, eager to buy homes. Expensive homes.

"A lot of people had savings when they moved to Nova Scotia. They probably don't anymore," Karr says. The development officer for Shambhala International laughs at this, but is serious, too. "It's not that easy to move to Nova Scotia from the U.S. You have to have resources. That was (made clear by) Canadian immigration — to get a visa, you have to be capable of getting a job, or have assets, or both. It certainly kept a lot of people from moving, people who would have loved to have moved, during that period of enthusiasm after Trungpa Rinpoche died."

A number of sangha members are extremely well off. By Nova Scotia standards, almost all are quite comfortable. Most settled in the fashionable south and west ends of Halifax; many found homes overlooking picturesque St. Margaret's Bay. But not all enjoy a high standard of living. Several dozen live in the less fashionable north end, the Gottingen–Agricola area, and Dartmouth. Still other members, including come-from-aways, live in small apartments and from cheque to cheque.

Shambhala International, meanwhile, is far from flush. It is, in fact, constantly trying to scrape money together. In the 1995 annual report executive council director John Rockwell, Jr. said, "Many of us, myself included, find that too much of our time goes into talking about money." Officials in most non-profit organizations talk this way, but few could go on to say, "Basically, our organization altogether is made up of volunteers."

It's common for non-profit organizations to pay their top executives $75,000 or more. Many, including the Izaak Walton Killam Hospital in Halifax, refuse to say how much their top people are paid. "The embarrassing thing with us is how little we pay, not how much," Karr says. "I can tell you what I make, because I don't care that people know I make $33,000 a year. And I'm the development officer and acting chief financial officer. The only person who makes more than me, other than the sakyong, is John Rockwell — and he doesn't make a lot more."

Karr's experience in the world of finance includes ten years in Paris, working with the prestigious investment bank, Lazard Freres. While there, he earned "healthy multiples" of his present wage.

"Shamhbala International has an average salary of $29,800, roughly. I'm including the sakyong's salary in the average, and it's not highly disproportionate." (Karr says $40–42,000 would be "in line.") "Plus medical, which is another $2,500. There are eleven employees: a few are part-time, which we add together to get this number. One is in Europe, the director of Shambhala Europe, whom we only pay part of; someone in Boulder is a development person for the Rocky Mountain Shambhala Centre; the rest of us are in Halifax. And these salaries are the result of a fairly substantial increase of a year or two ago. Few of us have any additional sources of income, and those are certainly not significant. You do it out of devotion."

Estimated 1996 spending for Shambhala International is just over $3 million. Shambhala Centre operations in the two largest and most prominent communities, Halifax and Boulder, account for about a sixth of this: $221,000 and $340,000 respectively.

Almost two-thirds of Shambhala International's money comes from donations and dues. All sangha members are asked to contribute to day-to-day operations. The expected amount varies from city to city, but averages $20–$40 a month. A fraction of income is derived from royalties, mostly on books and tapes. A full quarter of the revenue comes from programs, which tend to be expensive. Shambhala Training weekends start at $50 and rise to $120. This despite the fact that the overhead is cheap: practically all you do is sit quietly in one room. The three-month seminary at the Rocky Mountain Shambhala Centre is formidably expensive. The price for instruction, to sleep in a tent, and meals for three months is almost $5,000.

Total assets of Shambhala International, including properties, is $10–15 million. Debt is estimated at about $2.4 million.

Separate operations under the Shambhala International umbrella are almost always responsible for their own finances. Most operate on little money. The Vajradhatu Archives, in the basement of the Halifax Shambhala Centre, is a treasure house of information, and enjoys a reputation that far outreaches its size. Director Carolyn Gimian is also president of the 57-member Council of Nova Scotia Archives, and in 1995 presented a talk about the Vajradhatu Archives' cheap but efficient air cooling system at an international conference in Toronto. Yet shortfalls in donations have led the Archives to curtail whole programs. No longer does the staff include a photo archivist or someone working on transcriptions, and an audio recovery project of 10,000 tapes has been postponed. Expenditures for 1995 totalled less than $80,000, and the 1996 budget is $89,000. Including salaries.

Because of the paucity of funds, Shambhala events are often complemented by fundraisers. In the lobby of the Halifax Shambhala Centre is a five-gallon jug, ready to accept offerings of coins or paper currency — including Canadian Tire money. The plan is to keep it there until it has been filled twice, with the money going towards building improvements. The Rocky Mountain Shambhala Centre is financed in part by more than three hundred alumni giving an average of $15 a month — almost $60,000 U.S. a year. Still, an RMSC brochure features a full-page ad for Tibetan Hot Sauce, at $5.75 U.S. for twelve ounces. "Every jar of Tibetan Hot Sauce Helps Support RMSC!"

Occasionally, help arrives from an unexpected source. In the late 1970s Trungpa Rinpoche met Ganna Walska of Santa Barbara, Calif. They exchanged letters for several years and when Walska died in 1984 she bequeathed to the organization a collection of almost nine hundred pieces of antique Tibetan, Nepalese, Chinese, Japanese, Thai, and Mongolian art. After more than a decade of paying to preserve and store the treasures, the decision was made to sell the lot. In the spring of 1996 it was auctioned by Sotheby's of New York, netting Shambhala International $452,000.

Still, the attitude toward money has changed since Trungpa's death. While he had a tremendous ability for spending, he was also a genius at raising cash. He made exorbitant plans, with every expectation that the needed funds would arrive. Usually they did. But things aren't so lush anymore.

"It barely gets by, frankly," says board chairman Alex Halpern. "It's a lot of work to keep it going, and things get left undone until they become catastrophes."

"There are times of fat and thin," Karr says. "It depends on the goodwill of donors, and how they feel about the organization. The last decade has been very challenging for us. There's been a lot of distrust and concerns about how the organization was being run. It's been a period of fragmentation and donors have tended to target their donations to individual (activities) they believe in."

Like the Great Stupa of Dharmakaya. Built on a hillside at RMSC, the *stupa* is a ten-storey dome built in honour of Trungpa Rinpoche. It will house a huge shrine containing a large golden statue of the Buddha; inside the statue will be placed a relic of Trungpa's skull. A traditional Buddhist structure, the stupa is the sangha's current favourite project. More than $1 million has been raised.

Back in Halifax, Andy Karr says he doesn't regard the sangha as rich. He chooses a different word.

"Unmoneyed. I think we are wealthy, but not in the conventional sense of having lots of money and precious things. We're wealthy in people, in the teachings, the trainings, and wealthy in the ability to create an environment that expresses some sort of richness even without a lot of money. There are individuals in the communtiy who are wealthy, but not a huge number. For Nova Scotia we are a community of wealthy people, but by New York standards we're pathetic. It's not a rich community."

The international organization, Karr says, is in the process of making its income and expenditures more readily available to members.

"There's nothing particularly interesting to hide. We have been making an effort to communicate very straightforwardly. We haven't always done that, but certainly the current leadership is very concerned that we become more and more transparent, to our members and anyone else. In the annual report this year for the first time we published extensive figures on the budget for the organization. I think that's a good thing."

Shambhala International is blessed with a number of wealthy benefactors. Most, curiously, are women.

In 1985 Trungpa founded the Shambhala Trust, passing a hat among several wealthy members. More than $2 million was raised. But the money was gone within two years, with the last of it spent on Trungpa's funeral.

The Shambhala Trust was revived in 1995, by Sakyong Mipham Rinpoche. He invited several people, including some original members of the Trust, to a meeting at the Rocky Mountain Shambhala Centre. Again the hat was filled. But new ground rules were laid, too. No project would be fully funded, everyone agreed, since that could lead to erasing a sense of ownership on the part of everyone else involved. A rigorous evaluation process was needed to decide what to fund. And unlike the original Trust, which was run by the then-board of directors, this one would manage itself.

The new Shambhala Trust is geared to raise money only for capital projects, but its first decision was to donate money to operational expenses. Trust members, through an in-house letter, said they wanted to "change the perceived attitude in the sangha of distrust for the functions of our government, particularly financial." Because a new board of Shambhala International was just breaking in, the Trust offered to pay for both a financial officer and a development officer for six months, as well as partially fund the cost of legal restructuring, and the creation of a new data base including computers and software. In the same letter the Trust announced it intended to "not only help to establish funding priorities, but also create a sense of overview for areas such as education, family concerns, sickness and old age problems, and other areas not yet identified."

Trust members gathered in New York in December 1995 and Boston two months later to create a mission statement and written bylaws. They then offered funding to three projects: $220,000 towards establishing RMSC as a year-round, extensive practice centre; an unspecified amount to Dechen Choling, the retreat centre in the south of France; and $220,000 to help purchase a residence for the sakyong in Halifax (properties are now being considered).

No member of the Shambhala Trust lives in Halifax year-round. Maggie Granelli is here part of the year, but spends much of her time in Berlin. Four Trust members are in New York — Berkley and Bill McKeever, Arby Thalacker, and John Sennhauser. Pamela Krasney lives in California, Judy Robison in Indiana, Susan Dreier in Massachusetts, and Shanly Weber in Colorado. The sangha person perhaps most renowned for generosity is Trust member Martha Bonzi of Maine. When the Halifax Shambhala Centre on Tower Road turned ten years old in January 1996 Bonzi was there, and warmly received. As with so many Shambhala projects, her money went a long way toward making the dream a reality.

Martha Bonzi is a pleasant woman with a charming laugh. Clear blue eyes peer out from under a thick crop of grey hair. She's a grandmother in her sixties, and usually shy. A substantial family inheritance has allowed her to live without concern for making money, and give a lot of cash away. Before meeting Trungpa, she donated money to charities because, "that's what everybody did. You give because you've got more than you need." Since becoming a Buddhist, however, she sees giving money in a new light.

"One of the concerns of the Trust is to promote generosity as a daily practice," Bonzi says. "In the Buddhist community there are what we call the six *paramitas*: generosity, effort, patience, discipline, meditation, and wisdom. The philosophy is that generosity is the underlying thing that makes them all work. In other words, effort inspired simply by self-interest tends to be very harsh and non-inspiring to others. In a sense, the money is totally immaterial. A lot of what's going on is simply exchanging energy. This doesn't have to do with money; it has to do with making the world a better place."

The idea, Bonzi says, is that generosity can be a healthy part of everyone's daily practice.

"It does not involve just giving money," she told a 1996 Boulder community meeting. "It is the basis of all successful relationships. A person could feel that he is an isolated being, that there is no connection between himself and others, that his being ends with his skin, and then there is another being encased in *his* skin... sort of like animated sausages. But in reality there are connections based on generosity or lack thereof.

"You could say that we survive by a complex example of osmosis. Osmosis is the permeability of cell walls. How the cell is able to thrive or not depends on its ability to leak, both in and out. If the cell only lets nourishment in, and puts nothing out, it will be of no use to the organism and it will die.

"A community is like a group of cells. Humans leak. Have you ever shared a good laugh with someone? There is no sense of barrier. We crossed boundaries for a moment in an osmosis of goodwill. That is generosity. Basically the Trust was formed by several individuals who are not afraid to leak. We have come together because we would like to have our community, and therefore ourselves, thrive. We would like to share with you the limitlessness of generosity. We want you to appreciate your ability to leak."

Shortly after Bonzi embraced the study of Buddhist teachings and the practice of meditation, she made "a rather large donation" — widely believed to be $1 million U.S. Trungpa asked to meet her. "He scared the wits out of me," Bonzi says, laughing. "He had a sense of presence, an energy containing lots of stuff. I think the sakyong is getting to that point. But (Trungpa's) presence was just voluminous: it was like meeting the queen."

Bonzi was raised Episcopalian, in Los Angeles. "The reason I came to Buddhism is because there are no living (Episcopalian) teachers you can sit down and talk to," she says. "There's no suggestion you can go talk to your priest or whatever he happens to be and receive teachings. You can get the ten commandments and are supposed to figure them out for yourself. But there's no sense you could go to an Episcopalian school unless you're studying for the ministry. You can go to a Buddhist school with no intention of entering anything. Except maybe life.

"In Buddhism there is a philosophy, a whole range of things you can talk about, find out about. There is a way of coming in contact with who you are, of addressing your own mind, and becoming aware of it and its abilities.

"In the Buddhist way of looking at it, discipline is something that comes from within. It has to do with joy, it has to do with working with your potential in a way that you are having fun doing whatever it is. Discipline is created through a sense of generosity to yourself and what you're doing. If you're trying to play the piano for an hour a day and then one day you're just not into it, you might start out with something you really enjoy playing. It's not frustrating or aggravating, you can play it easily and it's wonderful. From that you can drift into the more exercise-oriented parts of practice. But the discipline gets accomplished because you've been easy on yourself. It's a very different approach."

Bonzi joined the sangha in 1983. A teacher friend, knowing her interest in philosophy, suggested she read the introduction to a new edition of *The Tibetan Book of the Dead*. The introduction was written by Chogyam Trungpa, Rinpoche. In it, he describes the various levels of consciousnesses, and how they get covered over by ego perception. Bonzi read it in the days before heading off on a drive across the continent, to California to be with her oldest daughter, who was about to give birth. She stayed with her daughter and grandson for two weeks after the boy was born, and in that time saw a remarkable change come over the baby. The ego was born.

"At some point I can remember saying goodbye to him," she says. "What was there originally was very open — there was no sense of ego, no sense of me, I. 'I need milk' or 'I need my diapers changed' or 'I need a warm spot to take a nap.' There was no sense of that: he was very open and a wonderful little child, really. (He's still a wonderful child.) But I realized that if I could have that sharp an experience from what Rinpoche said in the book, there had to be some truth to what he was saying."

On the drive back to Maine, Bonzi happened to choose a route through Boulder. As she arrived in the city via Interstate 70 she noticed her odometre reading 70,707.0. She thought it auspicious, and considered pushing her car to 70 miles per hour.

In Boulder she happened upon a sangha bookstore and was introduced to the first Buddhists she'd ever met. She went to the local centre to receive meditation instruction and, after a fast trip to tell children in Los Angeles and Oregon of her discovery, enrolled in programs at the Naropa Institute. Bonzi felt like she was coming home, had found something she had longed for.

"It's funny," she says. "All of my life I lived the teachings in an undirected way, naturally." Instruction deepened her realization. "It's supposed to be useful, a road map of how to live your life, basically. You have to live your own life, not someone else's life. You have to use your own mind. And it's not giving anything away — except the emotional quality which tends to whip you off your feet, that tends to take away from who you are."

She uses anger as an example. "If you can calm down from anger... your mind is clearer. If you get rid of the meaningless discursive thought so you stand in a clear patch, you can use your mind clearly. Meditation brings clarity, brings an awareness of who you are and why you do the things you do. You have to experience it. Otherwise the teachings are just somebody else's experience, which is meaningless to you."

Today, Martha Bonzi wouldn't say she's happy or content, "but I'm certainly more aware of my surroundings. If I practice a lot there's a great deal of clarity, of who I am and how I relate to other people. There's a sense of making sense of the world and addressing my potential." Her new understanding, she says, allows her to reduce boundaries between herself and others.

One of her four children followed her into Buddhism. "Then I have a sister and brother who think I'm nuts. A large number of cousins also think I'm nuts. But they're all sort of interested. I find more and more people are discovering the dharma and beginning to meditate. And that's what's valuable to me."

* * *

Sex

One thing has done more than any other to confuse, distract, and almost destroy the Shambhala community. Sex. A scandal in the late 1980s joined "sex" and "Buddhist" in the Nova Scotian imagination, and the perception lingers. Not only the community's reputation took a terrible blow; so too did its self-image. We are talking about the dramatic, public downfall of Osel Tendzin.

This is the one subject which many sangha members are uncomfortable talking about. On virtually any other topic, almost everyone is remarkably open and forthcoming. But the regent is a more delicate matter.

Partly this is because the whole fiasco did come close to annhilating the organization and setting back all the principles it stands for. Partly too some bitterness and diviseness remain. The sangha gets along better when it doesn't stare at who sided with who.

Trungpa was concerned that Westerners would consider his teachings to be foreign, so he wanted to indicate that a North American could teach them, too. In 1976 he chose as his spiritual heir a young Italian-American from Passaic, New Jersey, enthroning the former Thomas Rich as the Vajra Regent. Trungpa gave him a new name, Osel Tendzin (literally: Radiant Holder of the Teachings). Tendzin became Trungpa's right-hand man, groomed for the day when he would take the reins. (Osel Tendzin was actually Rich's third name — before meeting Trungpa he had been a student of the Hindu teacher Swami Satchadananda, who had renamed him Narayana.)

The transfer of power came with Trungpa's death in 1987. Less than two years later, *The New York Times* broke the news that Tendzin was dying of AIDS and was believed to have knowingly infected a male student, Kier Craig. The news sparked shock, grief, and fear in the sangha. The regent was famously promiscuous: dozens of people could be infected! To knowingly transmit HIV is tantamount to murder — the regent violated the Buddhist vow not to harm another being! After heated discussion the board of directors asked the regent to resign. He refused, on the grounds that he had been empowered by a lineage holder, so his position did not fall under the authority of a board.

What to do now? The community's Tibetan monk mentors in India were consulted, and on their suggestion the regent took a sabbatical of several months. He returned, however, not with an apology, but determined to retain his position. The deadlock deepened when he and some supporters moved to California. Many sangha members thought the board should resign for letting the situation get out of hand. How could it have happened?

The seeds of the disaster were in fact planted years before. Trungpa may have inspired thousands of people to practice disciplines which opened them up to experience life as sacred, but on the issue of sex he was a confusing example. His personal activities included fathering the present sangha leader, Sakyong Mipham Rinpoche, several years before giving up a vow of celibacy; and having sex with a great number of students.

Trungpa made it clear that sex was not something to feel guilty about; it was something to celebrate. Vajrayana Buddhism believes there is nothing wrong with sex — it's the craving, the attachment to sex which is dangerous. Anything can become the means for enlightenment and rather than avoid powerful or frightening subjects we should explore and work through them. The Shambhala teachings similarly hold that everything is sacred. "In some religious traditions," Trungpa said in *Shambhala — The Sacred Path of the Warrior*, "sense perceptions are regarded as problematic, because they arouse worldly desires. However, in the Shambhala tradition... sense perceptions are regarded as sacred. They are regarded as basically good. They are a natural gift, a natural ability that human beings have. They are a source of wisdom."

The active sex lives of Trungpa Rinpoche and Osel Tendzin are not exceptional among teachers of Eastern spiritual disciplines in the West. Jack Kornfield, in a 1985 *Yoga Journal* article, informally surveyed fifty-four Buddhist, Hindu and Jain teachers in the U.S., as well as their students. He found only fifteen of the fifty-four teachers were celibate and thirty-four — more than sixty per cent — had had sex with students. Some of these encounters were in the context of committed relationships that culminated in marriage, some were one-night stands, and some were affairs.

"It may have been easier to renounce and dismiss sexual questions in the celibate monasteries and ashrams of Asia, but as Western students and householders we cannot afford to ignore our sexuality any more than we can ignore the issues of relationship, intimacy, and emotions," Kornfield said. "Contemporary gurus and teachers offer few clear guidelines about the relationship between sexuality and spiritual growth."

Trungpa did not subscribe to society's sexual mores, but neither was he simply hedonistic. He insisted that honesty should prevail. Sleeping with someone other than your spouse was okay only if you were perfectly open about it, did not use coercion, and everyone involved could handle the emotional consequences. The point of being was being real, not debauchery.

Today Trungpa is joyously honoured in the sangha. The regent is remembered fondly by many and disparaged by others. No one believes that Trungpa or his appointed successor were charlatans, in the sangha solely to seize perks of power.

But the regent is widely considered to have been out of control — and out of touch with the teachings and basic goodness. He was renowned for his arrogance; Trungpa even mentioned the regent's arrogance in writing. A tale widely believed today is that on his deathbed Trungpa told the regent, "You can't die," and the regent mistook this to mean he was being empowered to live a long life no matter what his actions.

One longtime student described the regent's fall from grace this way: "Trungpa was brilliantly intelligent, the kindest person I ever met, and absolutely crazy. The regent had a somewhat similar mix of brilliant and crazy. The regent touched a lot of people in wonderful ways, which is why so many are still fond of and devoted to him. But his greatness and outrageousness were all wrapped up together and couldn't be separated. He wound up being torn down by an outrageous act." Another suggested: "Whoever Rinpoche had given the nod to would have crashed and burned and maybe sooner. Leadership is heady stuff. The whole sex thing, I think it's a symptom. I mean, who knows about that? That's not really what it was about. It was about what the first American asked to do this went through and how he ended up responding to it. And what that did to all of us."

Rather than proving that a Westerner could be empowered to teach Tibetan Buddhism and lead a community, Tendzin wound up showing that the Eastern devotion to leadership, mixed with runaway Western individualism, could produce a dreadful — even fatal — result.

But is devotion to a teacher always warranted?

In a 1991 article in the Vancouver magazine *Common Ground*, Katy Butler quotes no less an authority than the Dalai Lama as saying devotion to a teacher is not always warranted. "Too much obedience, devotion and blind acceptance spoils a teacher," the Dalai Lama said. "I recommend never adopting the attitude toward one's spiritual teacher of seeing his or her every action as divine and noble. This may seem a little bit bold, but if one has a teacher who is not qualified, who is engaging in unsuitable or wrong behaviour, then it is appropriate for the student to criticize the behaviour."

The regent disaster still reverberates through the community. Yet the old adage, "This will make you stronger if it doesn't kill you," applies. Members are now less likely to go along with a leader in situations they suspect are amoral and dangerous. They are more willing to accept that — no matter how powerful and wise the teacher — they are still oh so human. The sangha learned a hard lesson. Kier Craig died not long after the regent.

Things have settled down in the Shambhala community. The parties are not nearly so wild as a generation ago, and sangha promiscuity appears to be on a level with greater society. Of course, promiscuity was never a universal situation: many sangha members have never had an affair and have been monogamous for decades.

Sex in the sangha is made more conspicuous by the fact of the community's size. It can be a small world. Finding a partner inside the sangha is common; likewise if you are going to have an affair, that might be inside, too. The community appears to survive this with admirable good cheer. Many people would be uncomfortable going to a party where there are two former partners of your spouse, and two people you have slept with, and everybody there knows all about all of it. Of course, this situation can be found in any small community, including workplaces and most group of friends.

The difference is this: people who don't live by fixed rules have to go through the painful but rewarding experience of deciding the rules for themselves. Both the Buddhist and Shambhala teachings express the belief that life is complicated and multi-faceted and it's important to roll with the punches. Sangha members see past peccadilloes as just that — past.

* * *

The dorje kasung

At every major Shambhala event, and just inside the door of the Shambhala Centre on Tower Road, you will see uniformed guards at work. For day-to-day events they wear blue blazers, and look like flight attendants. For special events and at an annual ten-day summer encampment, they dress in khaki-coloured World War II-style military uniforms, and look like David Niven in *A Matter of Life and Death*.

Meet the *dorje kasung*. To non-sangha visitors, the kasung (literally: indestructible protectors of the teachings) often come as a bad shock. Though unarmed and instilled with the vow not to hurt another living being, members are taught military disciplines and use military language. Even within the sangha, the kasung is a controversial target of some derision. Militarism and spirituality are in some sense polar opposites: the first is based on aggression, the latter on loftier qualities. To have military personnel at an enthronement, funeral, or summer picnic can seem at least crass and possibly dangerous.

Yet the dorje kasung is an integral part of the Shambhala community. For many members, being in the kasung is the most rewarding part of their entire practice. Trungpa Rinpoche placed enormous emphasis on its development. Dorje Denma Ling, the retreat property near Tatamagouche, Nova Scotia, was purchased by the non-profit Dorje Kasung Society in 1990. The Society was established by the five highest-ranking kasung officials of the time — the sakyong, David Rome, Jim Gimian, Marty Janowitz, and Dr. Mitchell Levy (Trungpa's former doctor now married to his widow, Diana). Their main concern was to give the dorje kasung a summer home.

One of the five, Jim Gimian, is semi-retired from the kasung but still holds its third-highest position. A California native who has lived in Halifax for ten years, he says the dorje kasung is not what it may first appear.

"This is an extension of the meditation practice," Gimian says. "It's meditation in action. It takes what happens on the cushion, when it's just you, and puts you in the position of having to constantly deal with aggression as part of your practice.

"To my mind a lot of other teachers present Tibetan Buddhism basically as a religion — 'If you do these things you will be a good person.' That's not what Buddhism is about. Buddhism is about: you as a human being possess basic goodness. Everybody does. And it doesn't take mumbojumbo for you to understand that — it takes hard work. That hard work has to be as familiar to you as your blood, not something laid on top of you. And Trungpa kept trying to find ways to do that.

"Everything Trungpa Rinpoche did was to bring the potentially harmful, neurotic side, and the potentially good, enlightened side together. To make you understand they are not separate. This gets to a basic tenet of vajrayana Buddhism: you don't throw anything away. The roots of your neurosis are also the roots of your enlightenment. Your most hidden secrets are not to be run from. In fact, that's the root of the problem. You think there's something ultimately bad about you, and so you work to hide those things by fabrications, which we call ego.

"Vajrayana is based on going to those things directly and, by meditation, realizing they are just the essence of being human. By bringing them to light in meditation, they drop. You stop running away and become comfortable with who you are. Ninety-five per cent of the people attracted to Trungpa's teaching style will never be interested in going to (monastic) Gampo Abbey. Seeing that, he had to find ways that could speak the same truth. For hundreds of us, it was realizing aggression as something to work with.

"Trungpa Rinpoche once drew a map of North America. He said, 'Mexico is passion, Canada is ignorance, and the U.S. is aggression. There are three ways to ignore who we are. Everything you meet in the world you either want to ward off, seduce, or it's neither of those and you can ignore it. If ego is threatened, you ward it off; you can seduce it into affirming who you are; or you can ignore it.'

"The mentality of America was aggression. So the idea of creating a meditation in action that addressed the root of aggression was a priority for him. The distinguishing factor of Trungpa Rinpoche and his teachings was he took the gamble of trusting Western students' ability to realize their basic goodness. His task was not just transplanting Tibetan Buddhism or the Shambhala Teachings to North America, but to find in the West the forms that would express as powerfully the root of that sanity. In doing so forms were created, but they're not the way Tibetans did it. When we first went to the Tibetans and said, 'I'm a dorje kasung,' they laughed. Because in Tibet all they have is *kusung*.

"Ku is body, sung is protector. They have body protectors; they understand that. Ka is truth, dharma, the basic utterance of the truth. In the Tibetan religion human beings don't do that — disembodied spirits do that. In the early days the Tibetans heard what Trungpa was doing and didn't trust him because they thought he was crazy. Then they saw what we did, and how he taught, and they got it."

The dorje kasung were founded in 1974. When His Holiness the XVI Gyalwa Karmapa came to North America to visit, Trungpa realized he needed people trained in motorcade driving, bodyguarding, and crowd control. Trungpa had a passion for the British Empire, and especially liked British World War II-style uniforms. He had some imported from England and provided lessons. After the Karmapa went home, it was decided to keep the kasung in operation.

Since then, Gimian says, the dorje kasung have worked in concert with SWAT teams in most major cities in North America. When the Dalai Lama visited Montreal and Ottawa, kasung worked alongside the RCMP. At Shambhala community events they can be found sitting watchfully at strategic points at the back and sides of meeting rooms, at important doorways and entrances to the building. Disciplined, sober, and trained in attention to detail, they are ready to deal with crises including fire, medical emergencies, and verbal or physical assault upon a teacher. Lessons have been borrowed from the best bodyguard and motorcade schools.

Many sangha members treat the dorje kasung with the same mix of scorn and pity some people regard police. As with police, one bad apple can go a long way towards tainting the reputation of the barrel. Almost everyone in the sangha has a story or two about a kasung who, instead of being respectful, abused power.

Barry Boyce suggests that, while those occasions are true and regrettable, even they have a silver lining: the offending kasung then has to learn from, and deal with his or her actions.

"We could exclude all of these heightened, dangerous situations from meditation practice because we can always hire the municipal police or Mounties to worry about any conflicting situations," Boyce says. "But the dorje kasung says, 'Hm. How could we merge these teachings and our understanding of transmuting passion, aggression, and ignorance? How could we bring them together even in heightened situations when things get tense?'"

Boyce is a former head of the Baltimore-Philadelphia-Washington kasung, and now the fourth-highest ranking kasung internationally. In their day jobs, Boyce and Gimian are partners in the Halifax firm Victory Communications, a writing, publishing, and project management business.

"The strongest effect it's had on me is how I carry myself, how it's helped synchronize mind and body," Boyce says. "One has a tendency to treat oneself as a mind that has flesh it's dragging around. In the dorje kasung we have the training of standing and really feeling yourself on the earth. The uniform emphasizes that further — you have to notice your body. People look at you, you're a target. And you start whatever activities you do in that place, rather than in your head. So you pay attention, in a natural way, to extending your hand to someone, or any movements that involve guiding or helping someone. Movements of body or speech.

"If you watch a bouncer, his bodily manifestation is basically The Hulk. This is what they are communicating with their body. But in the dorje kasung, I've gone from sort of The Hulk approach, to one of being very relaxed in my body, and how I approach someone is to give them a lot of space. How you hold your body has an effect on how people approach you. We teach kasung in these areas: body, speech, and mind."

Martial arts also focus on bringing mind and body together to form one powerful force, and decree that members dress uniformly. Gimian says the uniform principle "is part and parcel of the transmission of the heart of Shambhala and Buddhist teachings to the Western World, addressing questions like how we deal with our own aggression. When you put the uniform on, you are already beginning to conjure up your own apprehensions and fears. It's an almost visceral reaction against all the harm that's been done by military and uniforms throughout history — it's ugly and terrible. You start experiencing your own connection to that and you are anxious about not falling into that pattern.

"Wearing a uniform, both physically and psychologically, makes you carry yourself with a very erect posture. The uniform principle was the way Trungpa Rinpoche transplanted the monastic tradition to the Western World, to directly address the Western mentality. Trungpa Rinpoche thought the dorje kasung was something Westerners could do, wearing Western clothes, to bring meditation in action to the forefront of every activity."

"In doing drill, you realize how much creative power human beings have," Boyce says. "People have tremendous potential to work for good if we synchronize our minds and bodies, instead of trying to battle each other. The drill practice is heightening the natural grace of the walk, but you have to discipline yourself."

"When soldiers do drill it's a completely different thing," Gimian says. "They are being beaten into submission in order to work as a unit. We are trying to bring out everybody's individual wisdom. They try to beat that out of them; our job is to get everybody to discover it. It's the same means, but there's nothing wrong with the means."

The means does not include weapons, Gimian says. But again, the style is similar to the armed forces.

"The dorje kasung has never had any formal weapons training or carried weapons as part of their duties," he says. "But the weapon principle is a profound element within our training.

"The only experience I have in and around weapons is, on a regular basis, perhaps as much as annually, a group of us would go out shooting, and many times with Trungpa Rinpoche. The point of that was to transmit that sense of power and danger combined in the gun. If you shied away from that and said you were not going to have anything to do with guns, it would be like not bringing some part of your psychological makeup to meditation. I've shot Uzis, and I owned a handgun, a 9mm that was given to me as a gift, as a symbol of weapon. It was given to me by some of my colleagues when I was elevated to the position I held, but I never carried it.

"Trungpa Rinpoche oftentimes spoke about weapon principle. He said it carried great power that you had to include in your meditation and you had to realize was the seed of neurosis and wisdom. You couldn't shy away from it and you couldn't get totally into it. The brush he talked about mostly, but the pen he considered one of the great weapons of all time, because of the power of the written word.

"Going out with Trungpa Rinpoche was an acknowledgment that it was okay to explore the weapon principle, in a disciplined way and an outrageous way at the same time. Disciplined in the sense that we had among us a member who had been in the Korean War and had strict training about the rules of a shooting line, how weapons are handled and loaded. Outrageous in the sense that we were there with a Buddhist/Shambhala religious guy who came from robes in a monastery and here we were shooting Uzis at targets! And he had a gun collection. I saw Colt Pythons — coolest weapon I ever shot, because it was a big heavy thing but really had tremendous accuracy.

"It allowed me to go back through that growing-up sense I had of fascination with the power of a weapon, and the fear of what was represented in my urge to kill things. It allowed me a space to hold both of those. It wasn't like throwing beer cans up in the air and it wasn't like just going out with buddies. It was with my teacher, around whom I always had to exercise heightened awareness. I brought the fullness of my mind to shooting a dangerous thing.

"Going through that a number of times, I felt that I learned to respect it. So many people have been killed and harmed by weapons! If we are ever going to take the human race beyond killing each other... I felt I had to experience that power and respect — and my own fears — in a sacred kind of environment.

"Trungpa Rinpoche would not shy away from any means it took to transmit basic goodness or awakened state of mind to anybody he met. So oftentimes he did things that seemed out of the bounds of normal decorum. And this, guns, is one of the things that didn't fit with being a Buddhist teacher. But, if anything, he erred on the side of trusting us enough that we could regard it as a sacred experience, and not giving a shit about the people who would criticize it and not understand. The foremost thing in his mind was, 'What is it going to take to have people get it?' With some people it was talks; with some, flower arrangement; some, a slap across the cheek at the right time, or going out and having a drink. He didn't shy away from whatever it took."

The kasung attracted FBI attention in the mid-1980s. Tracing local ammunition sales in preparation of a speech by then-vice-president George Bush in Fort Collins, Colorado, the nearby Rocky Mountain Shambhala Centre was visited by FBI agents seeking answers. They were invited in, given a full explanation, and were satisfied.

That's more than can be said about some sangha members. Despite serious apprehension among many of his own students, Trungpa put a great deal of energy and time into building up the dorje kasung. Every summer beginning in 1978 he hosted a kasung encampment — ten days of living in tents, training, and war games. For three years in the early 1990s the encampment was held in Tatamagouche, Nova Scotia. Before and since, it's been held in Colorado. The greatest number of participants was 325 in 1984. Trungpa was on retreat that year and encampment was the only event that prompted him to come out and teach.

Jim Gimian says encampment can be physically, mentally, and emotionally challenging. He recalled one episode in particular, when Trungpa took everyone up up into the mountains and divided participants into rival sides.

"We were sort of playing capture the flag, throwing flour in napkins wrapped with a rubber band. People would yell, 'You're dead,' and then break down and cry because they really felt what it was like to kill someone. I mean, it was out there! And afterwards Trungpa Rinpoche graded everyone, and he gave them zero or one out of ten. And he gave a talk, saying, 'Our purpose is to rewrite *The Oxford English Dictionary* so the word 'war' will come to mean victory over aggression.' Later he refined it, saying our motto should be 'Victory over war.' And it was raining and thunder, and all of these people were crying, and he took his weapon, a gun, and fired it in the air. And all of these people were at the verge of their existence, basically, and here is Trungpa saying, 'We're going to rewrite *The Oxford English Dictionary*.' And he made everybody switch sides, and go out and do it again."

The present leader of the Shambhala community, Sakyong Mipham Rinpoche, as a teenager. *Photo: Vajradhatu Archives.*

Children at the Shambhala Elementary School in northend Halifax receive a visit from Sakyong Mipham Rinpoche. *Photo: © Marvin Moore.*

Trungpa Rinpoche with his son, Sakyong Mipham Rinpoche, and the sakyong's mother, Lady Konchok. Their meeting in Colorado in the summer of 1986 was the only time the three were ever together. *Photo: © Diana Church*

Shambhala International executive council director John Rockwell, Jr. in his Halifax office with visiting Tibetan monks. *Photo © Diana Church.*

The principle directors of the Halifax Shambhala Centre. From left: Shambhala Training director David Burkholder, Shambhala Centre directors Moh Hardin and Shari Vogler. *Photo: Paul Darrow, The Daily News.*

Members of the dorje kasung eye their charges during a talk by visiting Tibetan monks at the Rebecca Cohn Auditorium in Halifax. *Photo: © Marvin Moore.*

The Regent Osel
Tendzin, in front
of his personal
banner.
*Photo: © Marvin
Moore.*

The cremation of the Regent Osel Tendzin, Rocky
Mountain Shambhala Centre, 1990.
Photo © Marvin Moore.

Sakyong Mipham Rinpoche doing morning exercises, attended by best friend Dana Fabbro.
Photo: © John Sherlock.

The spiritual leader of Shambhala International, Sakyong Mipham Rinpoche.
Photo: © Diana Church.

Chapter 8

The New Leader

"My father used to say to me, 'We're partners. We've been sent.'" The thirty-four-year-old spiritual head of Shambhala International, Sakyong Mipham Rinpoche, chuckles at this, piggybacking on the language of theism. "'We've been sent to do something, like some kind of mission.' This sounds kind of strange, but you have to have some kind of greater intention in mind to help people. If you don't have that fundamental desire, it becomes daunting.

"When we take the bodhisattva vow we say, 'I will work until all sentient beings have been liberated, have achieved enlightenment.' That's a very firm vow and commitment. When you think about it you think, 'Well, that is an impossibility.' And that is precisely the point — it's so fathomless that you give up having some kind of accomplishment.

"You just *do*."

* * *

The sakyong is good-looking, in an unusual sort of way. He has a shaved head, a high forehead, and a tic to the eyes. His skin is the colour of light cocoa. In official community gatherings the sakyong is treated with tremendous deference. He is greeted with bows and proclaimed by community leaders as "being the essence of wisdom and empowerment." He appears to take this with a bemused calm; knows the fractiousness bubbling behind the praise.

Is running Shambhala International fun? Sakyong Mipham Rinpoche laughs. "That's not the word that comes to mind," he says. He laughs some more; then is serious. "It's a lot of things. I have known all my life what I was being trained for, so it wasn't like I was a random choice. My father and I were not only father and son, teacher and student, but very good friends. We spent a lot of time together. I do this not because I have to, but because of my love and affection for him. Running this organization is very taxing. Constantly there are things going on; constantly you are working with people's hopes and fears. It's not easy."

The sakyong is not one to keep up a pretense. He talks openly about his frustrations with the job and the sangha.

"Sometimes when people come with me when I travel and teach, after two or three weeks they are exhausted and want to go home. I have to go for months and months. As well as teach, I have to work for the organization and think of the practical matters. Other Buddhist teachers who are Japanese, Tibetan, or whatever — they come, they do their teaching, and they leave. It's very easy. When I come in I have to do the teaching, the administrating, and deal with people.

"At the same time, I very much consider it practice for myself. If you start relating just to the things to do, it's a hopeless situation. It's not an ordinary kind of work. Sometimes I do feel like I'm helping people but other times I wonder, because I do things and then people don't do them, or don't listen, or don't care, or whatever."

The sakyong is personable, in an understated sort of way. He's a thoughtful speaker, making every word count. His sense of humour is subtle, vibrant, and often self-deprecating. Steeped in schooling of ancient and contemporary philosophy, he also sports an athletic side. He practiced martial arts and Japanese archery every day for years and has trained several horses. He also enjoys golf. "I never really played before because I thought it was, you know, a bourgeois game," he says. "But some of my friends in Nova Scotia kept encouraging me to play and here, because of the Scottish heritage, golf seems kind of low-key. So I play now and enjoy it."

He likes Mozart, jazz, and rhythm and blues, but not rock 'n' roll. He doesn't listen to music much — there's no time. His favourite pastime in spare moments? Studying Buddhist teachings. "I enjoy studying the dharma," he says. "Believe it or not, it's true. When I read a novel I feel like I'm wasting my time, even though it may be a good book." Although he rarely reads novels, a couple of years ago he did go on a Hemingway jag. "Hemingway I really enjoyed because I like writing. I felt I learned a lot about how to write, about how one expresses oneself. I've read different writers from that point of view."

The sakyong does read a great deal of non-fiction. Friends and associates say he has a voracious appetite for learning. He is known for being informed on everything from contemporary world politics to the history of chopsticks. When staying in hotels, he has a habit of switching on CNN.

His best friend Dana Fabbro says the sakyong "has a startling facility for recall. It's phenomenal. I've been with him at dinner and someone will be describing the nuclear energy system in France. After five or six minutes I'll trail off and start looking at the dinner menu. I don't know if he's hanging in there for every word or not, yet a month later I'll hear him recreate the conversation verbatim. He just has an unhurried mind."

The sakyong is a hearty eater, usually enjoying one large meal a day. He likes Italian food, Thai food, Indian, whatever's going. For breakfast he sometimes takes Western fare: omelettes, oatmeal, or pancakes. Almost as often he will take a Japanese breakfast: miso soup, vegetables, an umeboshi plum in hot water to make tea. He also enjoys *tsampa*, the national food of Tibet: roasted barley flour mixed with butter, and then with tea or water to make a dough. Like most Tibetans, he's a big eater of meat. Summing up his appetite, Fabbro describes his friend as "sort of a meat and potato lama."

The sakyong's love life, like that of any bachelor leader, is a favorite topic of community conversation. It's widely believed that, in the tradition of some Eastern leaders, the sakyong enjoys consorts. Fabbro says this is not true: the sakyong is a one-woman man. For several months in 1995-96 he was involved with a sangha member in Texas. "That's part of my job, too," Fabbro says. "He would say to her, 'We should meet each other during this time. Call Dana and find out how we can arrange it.'

"We've talked about kids a lot. I'm not sure how much he personally wants to do that and how much he sort of feels it's his obligation. For him, it's a loaded situation. It's not just, 'Hey, maybe I'll have some kids.' I think he realizes that at some point it's going to become another aspect of the whole circumstance."

The sakyong lives his life drawing on traditions of both the West and East. "He's very much Tibetan at heart," Fabbro says. "Culturally, he has a fondness and love for Tibet and India. But then you can't deny he grew up in the West and appreciates what he's learned and lived here. It was an important message from his father. His father adapted his teaching style to the West and didn't want him to return to the East to follow a traditional monastic lifestyle. He wanted him to continue the manner of teaching in the West that he had started."

Although not living the life of a monk, in the past few years the sakyong has spent a great deal of time in monasteries. After his father's death in 1987 he returned to formal studies in India and received a classical education, long on study, recitation, meditation, and prostrations. It continues. In the winter of 1995-96 he spent six months in Namdroling monastery near Bangalore, India, where days begin with chanting at 3 a.m. The monastery was founded by Penor Rinpoche, supreme head of the Nyingma lineage and a friend of the Shambhala community. The sakyong is treated especially well there: his previous incarnation wrote books that have been important in the education of many teachers at Namdroling.

* * *

The sakyong is believed to have been conceived in remarkable circumstances. Dana Fabbro describes it this way: "Trungpa was a monk and the sakyong's mother was a nun. Trungpa and Konchok knew each other and would sort of flirt. Apparently one night during the odyssey of their escape they spent the night together. It was a one-time occurrence and she was impregnated. That night she had a dream that she thought was very auspicious. She thought it would not be a normal child."

Trungpa and Konchok's one night together, in a Tibetan refugee camp in northern India, was soon followed by Trungpa heading to England. When he received word that Konchok was pregnant, he sent her letters, listing things he thought it important for her to do now. A visit to holy Buddhist sites was crucial, he said, and Konchok set out on the pilgrimage. The child was born in Bodhgaya, the same town where the Buddha achieved enlightenment more than 2,500 years ago.

How could a teacher reborn only to help people, and a nun, both with vows of chastity, have sexual relations? In Tibetan Buddhist culture, says Shambhala International executive council director John Rockwell, Jr., "A different logic is at work for tulkus. In some ways they are allowed to break rules, because people trust them explicitly. Much like a doctor is allowed to cut into somebody, so we allow them to do outrageous things that are conventionally against the rules. Trungpa Rinpoche was regarded as extremely unusual and gifted. In some ways, having his child would be a tremendous honour."

The boy, named Osel Rangtrol Mukpo, was raised in the Tibetan refugee area of north India until the age of seven, when he was sent to England to live with his father. It was a complicated transition: a change of culture and language was just the half of it. Trungpa had recently married Diana and some members of the Buddhist Society of London were furious. The year after Osel's arrival in England, Trungpa flew to the U.S. with plans for his son to follow. But a group of London Buddhists refused to allow the boy to go, declaring they believed Trungpa to be an unfit father. A custody battle ensued, resulting in Osel living in a children's centre for many months. Finally he was allowed to join his father in the U.S. but there, too, he entered an awkward situation. Suddenly he was living with a stepmother and a constantly changing group of his father's associates, none of whom spoke his language. The boy had a difficult time learning English; he was terribly shy, and developed a stutter. Sangha members shared the impression of a child who was sad and lonely.

Twenty-five years later, this boy is now the man the sangha is supposed to look to for direction and treat with respect. Not everyone does. Some members think the sakyong is evolving into a tremendous leader; others see a boy in monk's clothing, believe he is naive and his appointment was sheer politics. It's a tricky situation. The Shambhala sangha is not a group geared to blind devotion, and most who came to Halifax knew the sakyong not only as a child, but worse, when he was a teenager. Knowing someone through their teenage years is rarely conducive to later acknowledging their leadership.

"When we first met, we had a real fondness for each other immediately and a real passion for each other's energy," Fabbro says. "We were like a couple of racehorses. And a lot of what we did was just get together and vibe off each other's energy. We'd get together and drink beer, hang out, listen to music and just talk to one another. We'd talk about his father, or the regent, or the sangha, or Buddhism. We'd speculate a lot about what would happen when he was the leader and I was working with him. It was a little bit like kids role playing."

Fabbro and the sakyong (literally: Earth Protector) met in 1981, when both were 18. Fabbro grew up in Berkeley, California; his father was a Buddhist. The two friends have been together through rambunctious teenagehood and the confusion of early manhood to become crucial partners in the present and future sangha. Fabbro accompanies the sakyong around the world on official business, relaxes with him during brief holidays. He works as an aide: arranging plane tickets, reservations, meetings, and putting out minor fires. At the same time he is a trusted confidant. Perhaps no one knows the present Shambhala leader as well as Dana Fabbro.

"We spent a few years just tearing at the peep house together," Fabbro says. "You know, going to parties, driving around talking to each other, and just being completely enthused about the whole thing. The whole prospect of it was just so fantastic! After spending some time with his father he'd come out of the room, we'd take off in the car and we'd just be so energized. And he would say, 'You know, this (leading the sangha) is what I'll do some day. And you should be with me.' And I'd say, 'Of course I'm going to be with you. This is what we'll do. I'll be whatever you want me to be.' And he'd say, 'Okay, you'll have to travel, and you'll have to talk to people, and you'll have to take a lot of flak. People will really be on your case, and that's just the way it is.'"

Fabbro does not have an official designation, but both he and the sakyong know his unofficial title. Their first official trip together was to Trungpa's cremation in Vermont in 1987. Osel, then known as the sawang (pronounced sah-wong; literally, Earth Prince), asked his friend to come, but Fabbro was concerned that he would not be welcomed by the sangha hierarchy unless he had a title. "Okay," the sawang said, "you can be the SBF." That sounded good to Fabbro (the community has a penchant for acronyms). But what does it mean? "That's easy," came the reply. "Sawang's Best Friend."

Despite their closeness, Fabbro has never called the sakyong by his first name. He uses the traditional term of respect "Rinpoche," or the English "sir." "I just respect him. I have tremendous respect for the quality of who he is as a person. Even when we were teenagers, he used to say to me, 'Look, we're friends. You can just call me Osel; other people call me sir.' And I'd say, 'Okay, sir.' I just could never do it."

In order to earn the respect of the full Shambhala community, the sakyong has to overcome more than just being remembered as a nervous, stuttering child and hell-raising teenager. He stepped into the leadership position at the community's worst moment, when the sangha was imploding with fury and fear. The day after the regent died in August 1990, Osel Mukpo was appointed community head — by the Tibetans. Nyingma spiritual head Khyentse Rinpoche and Kagyu co-director Jamgon Kongtrul Rinpoche stepped in, and asked him to take over.

"They were the ones — and they were the only ones who could have done it — who said, 'Okay, it's time for the sawang to become the president,'" says board chairman Alex Halpern of Boulder. "He had been in India for several years. When things got messy, he'd got out of town. So he wasn't seen as taking sides."

The day the regent died, Osel was in Vermont at a study program. First things first, the twenty-eight-year-old came to Halifax, called the board of directors together, and asked them to resign. He explained that this was not meant as criticism — it was simply time to clear the decks. The board was so controversial it was best for all concerned if it stepped aside. The board did.

Next he sought to smooth over problems with the California faction. Accompanied by Halpern, board member John Sennhauser, and Boulder ambassador Rob Thorpe, the sawang flew to Ojai to meet the regent's widow, Lila Rich.

"It was a tense situation, but it was good that we did it," Halpern recalls. "It never became the problem it could have. The sawang had dinner with Lila — and they talked about the weather. But he did put his foot down: the picture of the regent should come off the shrine. What's on the shrines is prescribed. And his explanation was non-confrontational: we can't have pictures of everybody. We will have only Trungpa and the Karmapa. He tried to break down the boundaries between the sides, in order to heal the situation. But he made it clear that he was now the president, that there wasn't another Vajradhatu that was going to be led by followers of the regent. There was one Vajradhatu, and he was the head of it."

The Ojai centre did not remove the regent's photo from the shrine for some time but eventually the situation, with less rancor than most people expected, was defused.

(Records show that Lila Rich in one five-month period in 1991 received a payment of $17,500 — a sum that works out to $42,000 a year. Acting Chief Financial Officer Andy Karr says Rich was being compensated for her time as executive director of Shambhala Training, and no longer receives payment. "I think it was agreed Lady Rich would get money for a certain period of time," Karr said. "Along with the fact we don't pay very good salaries, we don't have pensions or anything like that. So a lot of these become ad hoc arrangements.")

"He doesn't do that much, but he's smart," Halpern says of the sakyong. "He understands what is important and is not important. He has one brilliant idea a year. I might have two dozen mediocre ones, but I need that one brilliant idea because then you have that sense of guidance to the whole siutation."

The potential fracture averted, the sawang got on a plane and began nine months of travelling from community to community: seven months to visit all the U.S. centres, followed by two months in Europe. In 1991 he described the sangha as being like Iraq (recently bombarded by U.S.-led forces in the Gulf War). The buildings were all there, but the infrastructure had been destroyed.

Some sangha members feared the community would fall apart as the sawang took the wrath of all the grief and anger. Instead, the new leader treated 1991 as a year of rebirth, appointing new people to leadership positions in almost every spot of the organization. Some people left, but the departures did not become a flood.

"It was a tour for him to find out where we all stood as a family," Fabbro says. "A dysfunctional family. We'd all been through so much; the organization had pretty much come apart at the seams. He didn't come out and say, 'I'm your new teacher.' He was saying, 'Okay, we're a family. Who are the cousins, the uncles and aunts? Who wants to do something else?' He was feeling the strengths and weaknesses of the organization and people. Also he was meeting people, finding out who the co-ordinator of the Milwaukee centre was. Did he know them? Did they still want to do this? It was a diagnostic sort of trip."

Given the terrible circumstances of his coming into the leadership, the new, untried leader might have been expected to make no major decisions for a few years. Instead, less than two years after taking over the sakyong defined the direction of the organization. In 1992 he declared that Vajradhatu, the Shambhala teachings, and the Nalanda arts would from now on operate under one name — Shambhala International. He chose the name because, to his mind, Shambhala vision encompasses all of the sangha traditions.

"It is important to understand the notion of Shambhala vision clearly," he has written. "Shambhala vision is not just that of Shambhala Training; nor is it that of mahayana or vajrayana Buddhism. It is a fundamental view that encompasses all of the various traditions. If we are practicing Shambhala Training, while maintaining our own ground we also need to realize that (Trungpa Rinpoche) was a Buddhist. He was raised and educated in that way. However, he propogated the teachings of Shambhala Training because that is what is needed at this particular time to raise the dignity of individuals."

As far as Buddhism goes, the sakyong does not emphasize esoteric vajrayana material, but has appealed to the community to get back to basics and practice compassion. In the 1996 Shambhala Day address, given live in his pyjamas via a satellite hookup from India, he suggested, "even though we are a Shambhala and vajrayana community, I would like to see greater emphasis on the hinayana attitude and the mahayana view of how we regard ourselves as a community and individuals." In Halifax in May 1996, he built on this idea. "Some people are attracted to the path because it makes sense, because of its philosophy," he said. "Others because they are hurt or hurting. But after they find this thing that is real and precious, they want to sit away from the world and be with that. You need compassion to go back in. It's not easy. It's hard."

He is also hoping to influence the community so that it spends less time bickering. "When human beings form groups, committees or councils," he has written, "there is sometimes an unusual or baffling result. The individuals are no doubt brilliant and compassionate people, but somehow, as they start trying to work together as a group, their wisdom and insight diminishes and indecision and confusions arise. This comes about when people are insecure, and the level of trust and understanding within the group is weak. So let us not fall into the pitfalls of trying to undermine one another, or constantly trying to shift our burden. Instead we must develop a natural sense of humour, which is fundamentally being open and letting go."

He has reason to be concerned. For the past six years, the sakyong has pretty much done everything his way. Time was spent figuring out who to trust, and on which strengths to build. Now, though, he feels the time has come for him to delegate more responsiblities. Despite the inherent danger.

"When my father was running the organization he delegated more and more responsibility, and it did create people saying, 'I don't like this person, I don't like that person.' But if he didn't do it, things wouldn't have grown. If it were just him, he would have had to run around even more, and his life would have been even shorter. Since I've been in his position I haven't delegated and precisely for that reason. I don't want to factionalize people or have people say I'm making favorites, so I've pretty well kept it to myself. Also, I need to trust people, and I needed some time to learn about them so I can trust them.

"I think it is difficult to put responsiblities on people and have everybody accepted, but if you don't do that people can be disheartened. It's like saying they are not able to do it but you are... So this kind of growing has to happen in the West, if it's to survive."

The sawang led for five years before being formally enthroned as sakyong, the community leader. "The first five years was like we were living together but not married," says John

135

Rockwell, Jr. "The community was still recovering from the previous debacle. The sakyong was rebuilding the community and the community was not ready for an official ceremony. It took five years to be strong enough."

The official enthronement of the sakyong as head of Shambhala International took place in May 1995 in a lavish, six-hour-long ceremony in Pier 23 on the Halifax waterfront. He was invested as leader by His Holiness Penor Rinpoche, supreme head of the Nyingma lineage, the oldest school of Tibetan Buddhism. During the ceremony, Penor Rinpoche also performed a blessing for the people and land of Nova Scotia, a *Kalachakra* (Wheel of Time) for Enlightened Society. Two thousand people, mostly sangha members from thoughout the U.S., Canada, and Europe, attended the ceremony.

"That was a huge event for him," Fabbro says. "He's an inscrutable chap and has always played his cards close to his chest, but he definitely noticed. For the whole event to be held in Halifax I think made him really happy. Trungpa Rinpoche recognized this place as having particular qualities and the sakyong felt that having it here was really appropriate somehow. Taking the enthronement from His Holiness Penor Rinpoche was also something his father wanted him to do. It was something he was prophesied to do. In the first few months of his life his father, who had left India by that time, wrote his mother some letters prophesying the child would be an incarnate child. Growing up in the West this has always been his life and destiny, to be a dharma teacher. The basic ground of his life has always been that he is a bodhisattva, reborn to do this."

Children of Buddhist teachers are often proclaimed tulkus, incarnations of important teachers. Trungpa was right. Shortly after his birth Osel Mukpo was recognized as the incarnation of Mipham Rinpoche (1846-1912). Trungpa, following a Kagyu lineage tradition of fathers naming sons as spiritual heirs, later proclaimed his son to also be an heir to the Shambhala teachings. The sakyong today is a lineage holder in two of the four schools of Tibetan Buddhism, plus the Shambhala teachings. Upon his enthronement, the Sawang Osel Mukpo became the Sakyong Mipham Rinpoche. Earth Prince became Earth Protector.

Trungpa's students usually offer astonishing superlatives to describe their teacher. "Other-worldly." "Overpowering." "The most amazing man I could hope to meet." Fabbro thinks that in twenty years people will say the same things about the sakyong.

"I didn't always think that. Trungpa Rinpoche is a tough act to follow. An impossible act to follow. Even by the standards of great teachers in Buddhism he's regarded as one of the phenomenal individuals. But the more time I spend with the sakyong, the more I've seen him willing to expose himself and be open, the more I think he's going to be a great teacher. I think in a lot of ways he's a good teacher now. Not so much in scholarly approach, but in his openness — the way he relates to people sincerely.

"Older students of Trungpa Rinpoche feel like no one could ever be like he was. 'The sakyong may be something else, but he won't be that.' Younger students, in age or experience, who are the sakyong's students and see him as their principal teacher, sometimes tell me *he's* phenomenal. It's all very relative."

* * *

In the summer of 1986 Trungpa suddenly decided the time was right for the sawang to see his mother. It had been sixteen years; the boy was now twenty-three. Trungpa himself had not seen Konchok since before their son was born.

Over the years the sawang had wanted to see her, and letters were exchanged. Trungpa had agreed they should get together, but never quite made the arrangements. She had been in India the whole time, had married and had another son, Gyurmey Dorje. She had never been on an airplane, rarely if ever travelled in a car.

When Trungpa got in touch he discovered Konchok was ill. So the sakyong flew to India, and took his mother to Hawaii for an operation. She went on to recuperate at the Rocky Mountain

Shambhala Centre and there finally again met Trungpa Rinpoche. It was just weeks before he would slip into the coma that would end his life.

Konchok today lives at Karme Choling, the retreat centre near Barnet, Vermont. She lives a pious life, is up early every morning chanting in her room, has breakfast, goes for a walk, and visits Trungpa's cremation site. Then it's back to her room to practice and study.

The sakyong and his half-brother met each other for the first time in early 1996. Gyurmey, now 21, lives in the Tibetan area of north India. He had just finished a three-year Buddhist retreat, and made the trip south to Bangalore accompanied by his father, Konchok's husband, Lama Pema Jelpo.

* * *

In the summer of 1993, the sawang spent some retreat time in Tepoztlan, Mexico. He emerged with a remarkable nine-page document outlining his view of Shambhala Vision. In it, he spoke his mind on major themes including the message of life, the esoteric teachings, and the community's mission.

On the sangha mission: "What we have here is not just simply a product of a single man (Trungpa). He used to say it was his 'duty'; likewise, it is now our duty. So let us not create a world that becomes so complicated and burdensome, like the yoke of an ox, that we ourselves can barely stand to be in it. I don't think anybody wants that. We must keep things fresh and interesting, traditional and new. And we must always be aware: we are simply trying to create a situation in which joy and happiness have an opportunity to raise our head and shoulders."

On the secret teachings: "As we progress in any journey, the teachings that are introduced as the higher or secret teachings, the profound teachings, are usually not obsolete and complicated rhetoric. They are simple, sometimes so simple that we fail to see the profundity in them. The process of understanding this simplicity and profundity can only happen when we actually relax — when we can relax, appreciate the simple day-to-day events of life, the little innuendoes, the basic dignity and warmth that each individual possesses and has the potential to cultivate."

On the message of life: "This vast and fathomless landscape that we have tried so diligently and so painfully to acquire," he wrote, "brings us nothing but an awkward and overwhelming burden. There might be occasional moments and glimpses of joy and happiness, but they themselves bring about their own demise when we try to proclaim some kind of solidity to our transitory pleasure. At each turning, a strong, persistent breeze attempts to remind us that life is a long and steady unfolding of a simple message of letting go."

Critics say the sakyong's reiteration of basic principles is proof of his lack of depth. The sakyong's emphasis on compassion and simplicity is not what the sangha old guard is used to. They were kept on their toes by the power and vision of Trungpa, by his twists and full-bore plunges, by the fact that anything could happen. Some miss those days desperately. The new leader is not the old leader.

Asked to describe his friend in a few words, Fabbro offers these: "Honest. Dignified. Joyful. Intimidating. He can really be like a mountain sometimes. He doesn't take and he doesn't give: he just is. Sometimes when you encounter that kind of steadfastness it's a little bit intimidating, because you see all your thoughts swirling around in front of you."

The sangha's slow and steady rebirth under the sakyong's unflashy leadership is earning him some respect. Dana Fabbro says his boss is a man of gentle power and tremendous insight, who will eventually receive the admiration he deserves.

"He's said on a number of occasions, 'If you lead a good, productive, wholesome life, I don't care what you call yourself: a Buddhist, a Shambhalian, a Muslim, a Catholic, a Christian.' He sincerely means that. Because if you lead a wholesome life, you will have a wholesome effect on other people.

"He seems to be getting deeper. It's like watching a bird soaring in the sky, and he just keeps going further and further, but effortlessly. By effortless, I mean the quality of his mind. If he studies a Tibetan text, he really studies it. He'll sit down for hours and hours, read it, think about it, talk to teachers, really study it. At the same time there's a way that he relaxes with what he's doing that doesn't create conflict. If you sit down to learn the piano, you're so uptight about getting it right and so critical of making mistakes that tension gets in your way. There's a quality in him that I've always noticed — he can stay loose and focused at the same time.

"He has his supporters and detractors, and the weight of it is a burden. He understands what his father's message was, and now there are things he wants to do. Changing the emphasis of the organization to Shambhala, for example. That's huge.

"Scores of people have said, 'You can't do it, it will never work, it's not what your father wanted.' And scores of people say, 'It's innovative, wonderful, and completely in line with what your father was doing.' Or, 'It has nothing to do with what your father did, but I see your wisdom and I have faith in that.' He hears those camps and then comes back to himself, and trusts his heart or instinct, intuition or wisdom. And then he carries on. He's got his hands full."

Chapter 9

World Headquarters

In the leafy south end of Halifax, on a picturesque street lined with Victorian homes, is the local Shambhala Centre. In fair weather the Shambhala flag and the flag of Nova Scotia are posted on either side of the door to 1084 Tower Road. No matter the weather, it's a busy place. Daily events include meetings and meditation practice; at least twice a week there are public talks. The three-floor, twenty-five-room building contains meeting rooms, multipurpose rooms, offices, and a shrine room suitable for community events including weddings and funerals. A former Knights of Columbus Hall, the building has served as the Shambhala Centre since 1986.

But it is not just a community Shambhala Centre. Downstairs are the organization's extensive, professionally-preserved archives. Upstairs are the offices of Shambhala International, and most of the people who oversee Shambhala operations in the U.S., Europe, Latin America, and elsewhere. In this building, too, is the urn containing the ashes of Chogyam Trungpa, Rinpoche. Once a year, during the April 4 ceremony marking the anniversary of his death, the urn is placed on the shrine room altar. The Halifax Shambhala Centre doubles as world headquarters.

***

Shambhala International comprises fewer than five thousand people — together its members would barely half-fill the Halifax Metro Centre. Yet it needs the structures, procedures, and systems of a huge organization. To do this, it draws on principles of both East and West.

Like countless organizations throughout the Western World, a board of directors and an executive council provide leadership and work on a myriad of day-to-day details. Yet Shambhala International is also headed by one person who is not hired or elected, but has the final say on any issue he cares to address. This, at least in modern history, is a much more Eastern philosophy.

Sakyong Mipham Rinpoche in six years has restructured the organization, introducing a name change and, in the spring of 1994, creating an executive council to work alongside the board. Shambhala International is now run by the sakyong, a seven-member executive council, and a fourteen-member board of directors. The board and council meet every summer for several days and emerge with recommendations for the sakyong, who usually ratifies them and makes a few comments. The sakyong also introduces new directions and sets the board and council to work on those.

"The sakyong's role in all of this needs to be clarified," says board chair Alex Halpern. "His father exercised yes and no over everything and was very much involved in administration. That's not the direction the sakyong has been heading. He's much more hands-off. When we reformulate the legal documentation I need to find out from him: does he want yes or no on everything. My belief is he will want that whether or not he exercises it — and in fact we would want that. In a way, that's his job. Because you have a board and an executive council, it's inevitable that we sometimes don't agree.

"If the board ever told the sakyong, 'This is what we think is the right idea,' and he didn't agree and he was firm about it, then we would do what he said. Otherwise, what do you have a sakyong for?"

* * *

Whenever Trungpa spoke in a new city in the early 1970s, he would turn people on to the idea of practice and study. The new students would regularly meet in someone's living room or basement; in Berkeley, California, the place to meditate was jazz drummer Jerry Granelli's garage. Only so many people could fit in such places and the sangha continued to grow, so in the mid-1970s a score of buildings were rented in cities across the continent. Trungpa called them *dharmadhatus*, (*dharma* meaning teachings, *dhatu* meaning space: space of the teachings). They were set up according to Trungpa's design. A co-ordinator ensured there was a schedule and good place to practice meditation and an executive committee oversaw membership and finances. Later Trungpa came up with the idea of ambassadors, learned associates he had worked with extensively, and he sent them out, one to each centre, as his representatives.

Trungpa called the entire organization *Vajradhatu* (Vajra meaning indestructible). It was charged with spreading the dharma, the Buddhist teachings. He created a second legal entity as well: the Nalanda Foundation. Named after a university built during a flourishing of Mahayana Buddhism in India, the foundation was established to promote the Nalanda arts. These explore a contemplative approach to art, education, health care, and psychology. Practices include archery, flower arranging, tea ceremony, photography, and T'ai C'hi. The Nalanda arts share the Buddhist and Shambhalian beliefs in discipline and sacredness in relating to the world.

Trungpa started the Nalanda Foundation in part because it enabled him to found the Naropa Institute, a degree-granting college in Boulder. Rules did not permit a non-profit educational institution to be part of a church; it had to be separately incorporated. When Shambhala Training came along, it originally was set up as a part of Nalanda.

Vajradhatu and Nalanda shared one board of directors: a dozen people, all of whom were full-time employees. Trungpa was president and chairman of the board. There was, not surprisingly, tension between farflung centres and the Boulder headquarters. As well as providing resource materials including tapes, transcripts, and teachers, Vajradhatu was fast becoming its own bureaucracy. Many people thought the organization top-heavy, and that the board conducted itself with too much pride.

Most board members moved to Halifax in the early and mid-1980s and had barely settled in when Trungpa became ill and, a few months later, died. The Regent Osel Tendzin and board carried on for another couple of years until the regent was diagnosed with AIDS and left in scandal. Twenty years after its founding, all of the organization's leadership figures were gone: Trungpa, the regent, and a strong, familiar board.

"When the preceding order came apart most of the centres entered into survival mode and began taking care of themselves independently," board chair Halpern says. "Connections were weakened. Some were in good shape, some were falling apart... We're still close to how it all comes out. In some sense, it's a semi-miracle that the thing stuck together at all."

* * *

Six of seven members of the executive council of Shambhala International live in Halifax. They have substantial decision-making power and are responsible for the implementation and running of activities. All seven have direct access to the sakyong and the power to operate without contacting him on a day-to-day basis. The council includes representatives from most of the prominent segments of the sangha, including Shambhala Training, Vajradhatu, the sakyong's office, and communications. All are full-time Shambhala employees.

Executive council members are:
• Director John Rockwell, Jr. A Buddhist scholar, he has a masters degree in Buddhist studies from the Naropa Institute, and is a member of the translation team.
• Andy Karr. Development officer and acting Chief Financial Officer. Looks after raising money and the membership program worldwide.

144

- David Brown. Head of the office of the president, personal secretary to the sakyong.
- Melvin MacLeod, editor of *Shambhala Sun* magazine.
- Jeremy Hayward, education director of Shambhala Training International.
- Diana Evans, head of practice and study for Vajradhatu.
- David Schneider, director of Shambhala Europe.

If the executive council is charged with the day-to-day running of Shambhala International, what does the board of directors do? At the first joint council/board meeting, a lot of time was spent on this question.

"This was a big debate," Alex Halpern says. "Is the board the boss of the executive council or merely advisory to the executive council?"

The answer came from upstairs.

"The sakyong said, 'The relationship should be non-dual.' By which we've arrived at: you have two reciprocal functions that need to occur. You could call it any form of dualism you want. Male and female. Heaven and earth. You have people who are managing, but they need to get feedback and response so that they remain responsible. It's not to say the board is their boss or has no influence and is merely advisory, but that on major issues the two must agree. There are things the executive council must understand it needs the board to be part of; the board's job is not to get mixed up in the business of managing."

Board member Barry Boyce of Halifax says that when the executive and board get together, it's not like one is reporting to the other. "It's more like the executive council comes to a semi-annual meeting of elders, so we can all look at it together. The board generally trusts the direction the executive council wants to go, but provides a broader view. The board offers advice. It's a work in progress and not yet clearly defined."

A new board was selected in 1994 and early 1995, with the final picks made in Halifax during the Heaven and Earth festival. Making the selections were executive council director John Rockwell; board chair Alex Halpern; Susan Dreier of Boston, who was retained from the previous board; Susan Skjei of Boulder; and, of course, the sakyong.

The board is an international outfit. Five of the fifteen members live in Nova Scotia, three in Colorado, three in New York, and one each in Boston, Indiana, California, and Germany. They meet two or three times a year, usually for four days at a time. The sakyong attends their annual summer meeting in Colorado.

The board of directors are: Barry Boyce, Larry Mermelstein, Deborah Ross-Webster, and Michael Chender, all of Halifax, plus Sharon Hoagland of Hubbards, Nova Scotia; chair Alex Halpern, Judith Simmer-Brown, and Susan Skjei of Boulder; Bill McKeever, John Sennhauser, and Arbie Thalaker of New York; Susan Dreier of Boston; Judy Robison of Indiana; Jeffrey Waltcher of Sausolito, California; and Rob Puts of Marburg, Germany.

* * *

While much of the day-to-day decision-making for Shambhala International takes place in Halifax, the day-to-day functioning of the Halifax sangha is a separate concern. To look after local affairs, the Shambhala Centre on Tower Road has two co-directors, Moh Hardin and Shari Vogler. Hardin is responsible for the Buddhist events and practices; Vogler handles all other operations.

Hardin was raised in Clemson, South Carolina, the son of a Methodist minister. He first bumped into Trungpa Rinpoche while reading *The Whole Earth Catalogue* — there was an excerpt from *Meditation in Action*. Years later, as a sangha member visiting Nova Scotia with an eye to moving up, Hardin found a greenhouse for sale in Maitland and opened River View Herbs. He sold River View to its present owners and moved to Halifax in 1988.

Vogler is a part-time nurse at the Abbie Lane and Nova Scotia hospitals. Her nursing background is primarily in caring for the terminally ill: for five years she was assistant co-ordinator of the Northwood Manor hospice program. She met Trungpa in 1975, when her immediate plan was to go to Korea with the Peace Corps. She never did make it to Korea; instead, she became a student and Trungpa's cook for the next ten years.

Vogler, Hardin, and a few others are licensed to perform marriages. Weddings are not frequent — there are usually four or five a year. Funerals are held in the Shambhala Centre, too. Usually the body is placed in the shrine room beforehand, so friends may meditate in its presence. Often at a funeral, readings, poems, and remembrances are offered. Sometimes ceremonies have special touches: when sangha member Beth Hunter, a Mabou schoolteacher, died in 1991, the Rankin Family came to the Shambhala Centre funeral to perform a Gaelic song. Funerals are conducted, too, for metro's Oriental Buddhist communities: mostly Vietnamese, Sri Lankan, and Chinese. Buddhist ethnic communities also use the Centre for major feast days like the Buddha's birthday (because of different calendars it falls on a variety of days).

Weddings, funerals, and other major religious events take place in the shrine room. The focal point of the Shambhala Centre, the shrine room is beautiful in an unexpected sort of way. For anyone more familiar with the glorious sobriety of a Christian church, the shrine room at first seems an almost cartoonish splash of colour. The primary colour is orange, representing wakefulness, and there is a liberal use of gold flake. Handpainted scroll paintings hang on the walls and there are two shrines: one Buddhist and one Shambhalian. Each is covered with dishes containing incense, rice, and other symbolic offerings. The shrines are not meant for worship, but to aid realization. There is no permanent seating; visitors scatter meditation cushions on the hardwood floors or sit on chairs in the back.

Two other people hold important positions in the operations of Tower Road. David Burkholder is director of Shambhala Training and Larry Loomis is Director of the Nalanda Arts. They join Vogler and Hardin on the Halifax centre's executive committee, which meets weekly.

Most of the Nalanda groups operate independently: each rents space from the Centre and looks after its own staffing and finances. Probably the best-known — and most dramatic — of the Nalanda arts is kyudo. It looks like archery, albeit with huge, two-metre long bows, but is not considered a sport. Instead, it is a five-hundred-year old Japanese code of honour, charged with concepts and beliefs aimed at building discipline and strength of character. The community is taught by local instructors and during frequent visits by Kanjuro Shibata Sensei, the twentieth-generation bowmaker to the Emperor of Japan.

At least twice a week the Shambhala Centre has an open house to which everyone is invited. Every Tuesday evening there is an introduction to Buddhism, a talk from 8-9 p.m. Titles of recent talks include: Work, Sex & Money; Fear & Fearlessness; Sense of Humour; Meditation in the Buddhist & Christian Traditions; and How To Be a Friend to Yourself. The talks are given by sangha members who are not paid but are selected for their expertise. It's an informal setting, usually with five to a dozen people sitting around a table.

Wednesday night is the Shambhala open house. Again, a one-hour talk is presented at 8 p.m. by a sangha member volunteering time and knowledge. It is always better attended than Buddhist Tuesday, with twenty to forty people showing up. The Shambhala talk is held in the shrine room, which opens at 7 p.m. for meditation.

There is no charge for either of the weekly open houses and everyone is invited to stay for cookies and tea.

* * *

Shambhala International is comprised of one hundred and seventeen centres in seven countries. There are four main types: full Shambhala Centres, rural practice centres, study groups, and forming study groups.

A forming study group means that a handful of people regularly get together to study Buddhism or the Shambhala teachings and to practice meditation. They are relative newcomers, however, and not yet ready to teach meditation to anyone else. Study groups are committed people who have been practicing long enough to publicize to the greater community that meditation instruction is available. They usually meet in someone's house or rent space in a church basement or community hall. A large step up from these are full-fledged Shambhala Centres. To receive this designation a permanent building is required, a variety of services must be offered, and the site must be consistently open.

All of the full-fledged Shambhala Centres were originally called dharmadhatus. Many centres are still known as dharmadhatus: to receive the new classification they need to bring Shambhala teachings and the Buddhist dharma under one roof, plus jump a couple of legal hurdles. Most have begun the process. Of the one hundred and seventeen centres, thirty-six are Shambhala Centres, sixteen are Shambhala study groups, and there are ten forming Shambhala study groups. Six are full dharmadhatus, thirty-nine are Buddhist study groups and four are forming Buddhist study groups. There are five rural practice centres, and one karma dzong (Buddhist Church) in the European headquarters of Marburg, Germany.

In Canada, Shambhala Centres can be found in Halifax, Montreal, Ottawa, Toronto, Edmonton, Vancouver, Victoria, and Nelson, B.C. There are Buddhist study groups in Annapolis Royal, Alliston, Winnipeg, and Kelowna, and a Shambhala study group in St. John's, Newfoundland. Thirty-two organizations are recognized in Europe. The continent has five Shambhala Centres, in Amsterdam, Paris, Hamburg, Freiburg, and Munich. In Latin America there are dharma study groups in Santiago, Chile, and Sao Paolo, Brazil. There are seventy-five centres in the United States.

Retreat centres are where members go for retreats and special programs. They are Dechen Choling in southern France; Dorje Khyung Dzong in southern Colorado; Gampo Abbey in Pleasant Bay, Cape Breton; Karme Choling near Barnet, Vermont; and the Rocky Mountain Shambhala Center, west of Fort Collins, Colorado.

Being a major Shambhala Centre or rural practice centre has its privileges. Centres can make requests for visits by the sakyong or visiting Tibetan teachers, and receive beautiful Shambhala and Buddhist banners made by Paul Hannon of Halifax. This year, thirty centres also received a small box containing bone relics of Trungpa Rinpoche. Designed in consulation with Tibetan teachers Thrangu Rinpoche and Tenga Rinpoche, they were put together at Gampo Abbey. Khyentse Rinpoche chose the pieces of bone to be used. The bone can be seen through a window in the reliquary: some members find understanding by meditating in its presence. The first ones were placed on shrines in Halifax and at the Rocky Mountain Shambhala Centre.

Rural practice centres are an important part of the Shambhala organization, offering places to stage large programs and to study and practice undistracted by daily events. The two most important are the Rocky Mountain Shambhala Centre (RMSC) in northern Colorado, and Gampo Abbey in Nova Scotia.

RMSC was founded in 1971 on four hundred acres of isolated, mountainous land. It's a fabled place among the organization, believed to be charged with special energy. The weather is exotic: brilliant summer sunshine can be followed by a hailstorm, lightning, and more intense heat. Wild animals wander in and out. At almost nine thousand feet altitude sickness is a problem, and coyotes can be a concern. Last year one dashed out of the woods and made a meal of a pet dog.

It is here that a three-month Buddhist seminary is held every second summer, matching the sangha's best teachers with hundreds of people who come from all over the U.S., Canada, and Europe. The first month is dedicated to hinayana teachings, the second to mahayana, and the third to vajrayana. Always, there is meditation. There are nowhere near enough buildings; almost everyone sleeps in tents. A large main building houses a kitchen, dining room, and shrine room. In the shrine room is a scroll painting presented to Trungpa by the Queen of Bhutan.

RMSC's legends began with its first sangha settlers. Trungpa asked a group of commune-dwelling hippies to live there and the pygmies — which is what they called themselves — moved in, without electricity, plumbing, or other modern conveniences. On the day they arrived neighbours sporting shotguns formed a welcome committee and advised them to leave, quick. Instead, they scratched out an existence, and built roads and houses still used today. A major motion picture deal was signed in 1980 to bring the story of the pygmies to the silver screen, but like so many film deals never advanced past the contract stage. Too bad: Charles Bronson was slated to play now-Halifax resident Don Winchell.

Gampo Abbey has the peculiar distinction of being both a Buddhist monastic community and listed in the travel guide *Fodor's Nova Scotia*. It's an idyllic setting, nestled on an ocean cliff just north of Pleasant Bay, Cape Breton. But the abbey is far from a resort. It is the first monastery in the Tibetan vajrayana tradition to open in North America, and the Shambhala community's only centre training Western men and women for the monastic path. It is financed primarily by donations; long-term residents pay $600 per month. Founded by Trungpa Rinpoche in 1984, it is overseen by Khenchen Thrangu Rinpoche, Abbot of Rumtek Monastery in Sikkim, India. Thrangu and Trungpa were boyhood friends.

The abbey's main building has living quarters for thirty people, a library, and a shrine room overlooking the ocean. Residents live in private rooms or dormitories. The diet is primarily vegetarian but includes dairy products and some local fish. Everyone on the premises shares in the responsiblity of cleaning and caring for the place.

Meditation, study, and contemplation are the foundations of monastic life. The daily schedule includes at least three hours of meditation practice, and the study of Tibetan and traditional texts are important parts of the curriculum. Everyone at the Abbey — all residents, workers, and guests, are required to follow the five Buddhist precepts: to refrain from killing, lying, stealing, sexual activity, and taking intoxicants.

The resident director is Pema Chodron, a nun in the Kagyu lineage. An American, Pema was born Dierdre Blomfield-Brown and as a young woman earned degrees from Sarah Lawrence College and the University of California at Berkeley. By the age of twenty-one she was married and had two children. After a painful divorce in 1972, she discovered the Buddhist path. Pema was ordained a novice nun in 1974 and received a full nun's ordination in 1981.

The monastic path has four stages. Anyone interested in becoming a monk or nun is first asked to live at the abbey for at least six months, either as work-study participants or paying guests. If all goes well they may then take pre-novice vows and wear robes. Following at least one year as a pre-novice they may take vows as a novice — thereby making a lifetime commitment to monastic life. Lastly comes full ordination. After at least two years as a novice, one may take the full vows of a monk or nun. These include vows of celibacy and abstaining from intoxicants.

Set off from the rest of the buildings is Sopa Choling, the abbey's group retreat centre. Thirty-two people are presently participating in a three-year meditation retreat. Because the demands — and expense — of living in retreat for three years is impossible for most Westerners, the thirty-two have been split into two groups of sixteen and are taking six-month turns at being in retreat.

Some people who spend time at the abbey, however, are not on a strict monastic path. The great majority go to attend a program, usually ranging from a week to a month in length. The programs usually stress individual meditation and study. Introductory programs are periodically offered and individual instruction is usually available.

Also in Nova Scotia, and regularly used by sangha members in Halifax, is Dorje Denma Ling (DDL). Located just south of Tatamagouche, it's a rural contemplative centre on nearly 270 acres of forest, meadows, and streams, offering a view of the Northumberland Strait and Prince Edward Island.

The site is owned by the non-profit Dorje Denma Ling Society, governed by a board of directors and managed mainly by volunteers. DDL annually hosts four family camps, a children's camp, and a Rites of Passage weekend for eight-year-olds. Recently DDL has been offered as a rental space to Nova Scotian groups who might not have direct Shambhala connections, but whose activities are consistent with Shambhala efforts and vision. Plans include a group of summer, retreat, and perhaps year-round cabins to be offered on long-term leases to families, groups, and individuals.

The sakyong has been a supporter of DDL, and a member of the society and board, since its founding. He named it, too: Dorje Denma Ling means Place of Indestructible Warriorship. The sakyong has also designated a meadow as a place suitable for holding Nova Scotia's first outdoor cremations.

Chapter 10

Nothing Happens

A bumper sticker popular in the Shambhala community makes this declaration: "Nothing Happens." It's an expression of basic belief. Because we are all impermanent, because reality manifests itself in myriad ways but in essence never changes — nothing happens.

This bumper sticker is ironic and funny especially when considering the Shambhala community's impact on its chosen province. In practically every field of human endeavour, the hard work of sangha members has made Nova Scotia a better place. It is impossible to tell the story of contemporary Nova Scotia without attributing the Shambhala community a leading role.

Sangha members have founded the Nova Scotia Sea School, the Great Ocean natural food market, the province's first mindfulness stress reduction clinic, and an internationally-selling magazine. They have opened bookstores, cafes, bakeries, clothing stores, organic farms, a branch of peer lending, and the one and only Italian Market. The community boasts architects, lawyers, venture capitalists, photographers, economists, university professors, software designers, even a golf pro. Members have made movies, directed Symphony Nova Scotia and the Discovery Centre, won house design awards, received a Progress Women of Excellence Award and an honorary degree from St. Francis Xavier University. They have headed the Council of Nova Scotia Archives, the Nova Scotia Film and Video Producers Association, NovaKnowledge, and the children's section of the Atlantic Film Festival.

Listing all these involvements would be a book unto itself. Here is just an overview of some prominent sangha members and their work in Nova Scotia.

* * *

Crane Stookey was a Boston architect when he decided to ditch the rat race and head for the open sea. For several years he served on schooners and tall ships sailing as far as Hawaii. Today, he brings common sense and exceptional skill to the problem of bored teenagers. He's giving them something greater than drugs, cooler than ennui. He's opened the Nova Scotia Sea School. "I'm not trying to build sailors," Stookey says, "I want to help kids grow up. Boats and the water are a magnificent teacher. You can't say, 'I don't feel like doing this today,' because you'll end up on the rocks."

Through the fall and winter months, under adult supervision, kids 14-18 experience every facet of boatbuilding. First thing, they head into the woods to select the trees to use in building a boat. Eventually they will sail that boat from Halifax to Lunenburg. The schools' first row/sailboat, the twenty-eight-foot Dorothea, was launched on Canada Day 1995. A second boat is scheduled to be launched in spring 1997.

"Young people, especially in urban areas, do not view the sea as part of their lives," Stookey says, "and are not learning from the wisdom of their seafaring lineage. Kids can learn something fundamental here, and it's something you can't learn by just being told. All young people need to be challenged, and being challenged in a group is an excellent way to learn generosity. If you're not challenged in a group, you grow less inspired to help others."

His efforts have been supported by organizations including the Maritime Museum of the Atlantic and the Canadian Armed Forces.

"I was very struck by the generosity of the Armed Forces. I called up and said, 'I hear you've got a whaler,' and they gave us the boat for nothing, plus a slip and a classroom. When I mentioned how difficult it was to get kids over to Shearwater, they said, 'Fill out a form, we'll requisition a bus.' That isn't what we did, as it turned out, but I was really impressed. Especially being from the States. Canada doesn't have the same level of assumed enmity, I suppose, so the Forces sometimes act more like public service organizations. Of course, boats are a good place to learn military precision. And if you take aggression out of the military there's a lot of good there, like the notions of discipline and honour."

Crane Stookey is teaching Nova Scotia kids valuable lessons. But it's not all about learning. "It's a blast," he says. "What could be more fun than building a boat yourself, getting in it and sailing away?"

* * *

For six years Marty Janowitz, a native New Yorker, has inspired Nova Scotians to take better care of the province. Under his leadership, the Clean Nova Scotia Foundation became a household name, and environmental concerns a priority. Fifty thousand Nova Scotians now get involved in CNSF programs to clean up the province's beaches and rivers every May — one in every eighteen people in the province.

In the fall of 1996 Janowitz left Clean Nova Scotia to take his expertise to the global stage. He joined Jacques Whitford, an environmental engineering firm promoting sustainable development, waste management, clean air and water in China, Latin America, and other locations. Janowitz is manager of the firm's environmental science group, communicating with scientists around the globe, with the aim of helping the group become more efficient.

Jacques Whitford is an employee-owned company based in Dartmouth. Private sector environmental activity, Janowitz says, has tremendous potential in the province.

"The missing link is how to make environmental concerns mesh with economic opportunties. There's a void between big makework projects coming from outside and a lot of the talents and energies we have right here... We're only beginning to realize the level of pressure on the planet. I'd love to see a Nova Scotia-based company in the forefront of a systemic redesign that's increasingly important on a global level."

* * *

"Basically, one's an immigrant on arrival," Basha Turzanski says. "How does one enter another society as an immigrant? A lot of immigrants start businesses, because it's a way to become part of the mainstream. We didn't want to be outside of Nova Scotian life but meet people, become part of daily life, and become Nova Scotians. The way to do that is to open your door and invite people in."

Basha and Ludwik Turzanksi had no experience in shop-keeping before moving to Halifax. In Boulder both were teachers: Basha taught psychology at the Naropa Institute, and Ludwik sculpture at the University of Colorado. Today they operate the largest health food store east of Montreal. Great Ocean Natural & Specialty Foods, on Quinpool Road, is a regular stop for thousands of Nova Scotians. It offers a range of organic produce, organic beef and chicken, herbs and vitamins, a deli section, local products, and thousands of imported foodstuffs. It has also earned a reputation as one of the friendliest and most informative stores in town. Staff is offered classes prepared by a naturopathic college in Washington State. Every month there's a free lecture by a naturopathic physician.

"Personally, it's not so much selling things over the counter that I enjoy but creating some sort of space that feels good," Basha says. "It's fun to create a space and an environment." The store provides for people with environmental sensitivies, in part by using non-toxic cleaning materials. A great deal of energy, thought, and money were spent on store ambiance. The colors and lighting are gentle, and walls are adorned with food murals by Tatjana Krismanic.

The irony is that Great Ocean is located in a former Sobeys grocery store. "This is not just making a living," Ludwik says. "We're trying to live our lives properly and help society."

* * *

Shops

Sangha members have opened a number of stores in Nova Scotia. Most are in Halifax, others are located in Mahone Bay and Cape Breton.

Best-known is the Trident Booksellers & Cafe, on Argyle Street in downtown Halifax. Attractively appointed in burgundy and wood, the Trident offers cappuccinos brewed by a machine so intricate it has to be calibrated daily to suit atmospheric conditions. The Trident is owned and operated by Hudson Shotwell and Janet Moe. One-half of the shop is a cafe; the other is a bookshop selling both new and used books. Its emphases are religion and culture. Trident buys thirty-three kinds of used books including Anthropology, Art, Architecture, Biography, Canadiana, Spirituality, Travel, and Women's Studies. There are eight kinds of publications it will not buy: Romance, Computer, Westerns, Reader's Digest Condensed, Textbooks, Magazines, and most True Crime and Horror.

The Trident is famous for coffee but almost as renowned for its muffins and chocolate-dipped oatcakes. These come from Paradise Bakery, a delectable shop on Agricola Street in the north end. Owner Norris Eddy created edible wonders at some of the city's best restaurants, including Fat Frank's, Soho, and the Silver Spoon, before opening Paradise. He had never before baked oat cakes, but decided to try because they are so popular in Nova Scotia. (The recipe, naturally, comes from a Zen centre in San Francisco.) Paradise is famous for friendly service and great food including spanakopita and foccachia, as well as pastries. The shop pleases its neighbours by staying open all night Friday.

Another popular food store is the Italian Market, on McCully Street. It offers a Nova Scotia-record seventy-five varieties of pasta, including angel hair, wagon wheels, and twenty-two-inch-long spaghetti. Opened in 1991, it doubled in size in 1995 to include a twenty-eight-foot-foot deli counter, a kitchen serving pizza and less familiar foods, tables for enjoying pastries and coffee, and the neighborhood's first cappuccino machine. The Market is a surprise to owners Gus and Kate Abato. Floridian Kate worked in Washington 10 years as a China analyst for the U.S. government; Gus, from Boston, was an insurance executive. They moved north with their two boys in the mid-1980s. It wasn't easy, and by 1991 Kate and Gus considered leaving. But then they heard that a little store they liked was for sale. Five years of hard work and calculated risks later the Italian Market is an institution, beloved by people who want to experience more of the world's cuisine. Customers come from all over the province.

Aerobics First is one of metro's best-known athletics goods stores. Owner Margaret Armour was a longtime Aerobics First employee who took over ownership of the store in 1990, when the bank was threatening foreclosure. She built it into a success, with ideas including creating a Friends of Aerobics First client card entitling cardholders to up to 30 per cent off some goods. From 242 members in 1990, the list has grown to more than 22,000. Armour's efforts have not gone unrewarded. She was named Canada's 1994 Woman Entrepreneur of the Year in the Turnaround category, by a business institute of the University of Toronto.

A native Haligonian, Armour attended all of the levels of Shambhala Training. "Shambhala Training added to my business skill," she says. "Partly because I'm more able to deal with stress. I see now that my whole world can be united: what I do in my work is as important as what I do in my spiritual path. They are basically the same thing. My interest is the need to build more enlightened organizations, to nurture attitudes like work-sharing, to have business see people as the most important part. I know this sounds like buzz words but I believe that even working in a small store, you can be the best that there is. That's what I believe and, my God, my staff believe it too."

Acadia & Quigley's Decorating Centre, just across Quinpool Road has tripled its sales since Paul Susnis saved it from receivership. A painting contractor in Boulder for eighteen years, Susnis moved into decorative painting when he came to Halifax. As well as own a store he has become involved with the movie business, providing knowledge and work for films including *Two If By Sea* and *Dolores Claiborne*. "I'm surprised to be running a store, but there wasn't anything in town quite like what I perceived as a full-service, painters' paint store," Susnis says. "We brought in gadgets and speciality tools I knew about and whatever else people asked us for and it snowballed. You can't get rich here but I've got five employees now, after opening it by myself."

The Attic Owl bookstore, on South Street beside the Victoria General Hospital, is a favourite of the university communities and southend bookworms. Owned by mother and daughter team Jan Watson and Fenella Ax, it also boasts one of the city's best selections of Buddhist and Shambhala books.

Jim Ennis operates one of Halifax's funkiest clothing shops. Blue Heron, in the heart of Spring Garden Road, provides shirts, skirts, and shoes for the decidedly hip. Ennis' beautiful house overlooking St. Margaret's Bay is sometimes used for major community events, including visits by the sakyong.

Drala, a books and gifts store, is operated by Charles Marrow on Grafton Street. It has a wide range of items to complement Shambhala and Buddhist practices, but most customers visit for the Oriental gifts and books.

In Mahone Bay on the south shore, Steve and Rita Armbruster have opened the Mermaid Cafe. It's in classy company, next to P'Lovers and the LaHave Bakery.

* * *

Health

Sangha members are particularly prominent in the health professions. The community includes psychologists, psychiatrists, MDs, midwives, massage therapists, homeopaths, and physiotherapists.

Several professionals joined together in 1989 to open EastWind Health Associates, on Windsor Street in Halifax. Early in 1996 EastWind psychotherapist Timothy Walker founded Atlantic Canada's first mindfulness stress reduction clinic.

"Our culture puts stress on us — nobody denies that," Walker says. "If you asked 10 people on the street, 'Is the average person stressed out?,' they'd all agree. And the human body is not built to go through this every day. It breaks down."

Doctors who discover their patients are sick with stress sometimes send them to Dr. Walker. He teaches patients how to focus their minds, creating a break from stress and helping them realize they have power to deal with their problems.

"Science is beginning to show that stress is hormonal, physiological — every system of the body is affected by stress," Walker says. "One of the most important things you can do is learn how to respond to stress in a healthy way."

* * *

Culture

The sangha is teeming with cultural talent. Artists include actors, painters, writers, musicians, musical instrument makers, dancers, and composers.

Most famous is Cathy Jones, one of Canada's best-known comedians and co-host of the weekly national CBC-TV show *This Hour Has 22 Minutes*. A Newfoundland native who now lives in Halifax, she regularly gives benefit performances for Shambhala organizations. In the summer of 1996 Jones married sangha member Paul Hannon, a painter and owner of Paul Hannon and Associates, a flag and banner-making company which provides the banners for sangha shrine rooms worldwide.

Peter Lieberson came to Nova Scotia to work as international director of Shambhala Training, but classical music lovers know him as a guest conductor with Symphony Nova Scotia. The son of the late Goddard Lieberson, former president of Columbia Records, and the ballerina Vera Orina, Lieberson is one of the most widely hailed composers of his generation. He has performed with a score of major U.S. and European ensembles, including Pierre Boule and the New York Philharmonic, the Boston Symphony Orchestra, and the London Sinfonietta. Most recently Lieberson completed the music for a film, *Warrior Songs*, with performances by Yo Yo Ma and Emanuel Ax.

Warrior Songs was shot in the summer of 1996 in Halifax and New York. It tells the tale of a legendary Tibetan king, Gesar of Ling, and stars Trungpa and Diana's oldest son, twenty-three-year-old Gesar Mukpo. *Warrior Songs* is produced by Halifax sangha member Lesley Ann Patten, who co-directed the CBC-TV special *The Battle for Moser River*. She operates her own company, Great Eastern Cine Productions Ltd.

Two other sangha members hold important positions in the province's growing film industry. Johanna Lunn Montgomery is director of the children's program of the Atlantic Film Festival, ScreenScene, the only one of its kind in Canada. Angela Gwynn-John is the Atlantic Film Festival's international programmer and former executive director of the Nova Scotia Film and Video Producers Association.

Other sangha cultural stars include internationally-renowned jazz drummer Jerry Granelli. He lives in Halifax part of the year, and always makes sure to be back for the Atlantic Jazz Festival in July. Tatjana Krizmanic is a painter whose work has graced everything from galleries to postcards. Miriam Garrett is development director at the Art Gallery of Nova Scotia and Sally Walker is executive director of the Discovery Centre.

Ruth Whitehead received an honorary Ph.D from St. Francis Xavier University in 1995 for her work as an oral historian with the Mi'kmaq. She has also written two books about Nova Scotia's natives: *Elitekey, Micmac Material Culture*, and *Micmac Quillwork*. Both were published by the Nova Scotia Museum.

Trudy Sable has worked for eight years to understand how the Mi'kmaq language and perception of reality work. Her Saint Mary's University Masters thesis considered these questions. "Instead of the European noun-centered view of the world, in which the world is full of objects that can be gotten hold of and taken apart," Sable says, "the world is in flux, is flowing." Her appreciation of native wisdom led to her being hired by Parks Canada to write a report suggesting how to increase the interpretation of Mi'kmaq heritage in the parks system. This inspired both Fortress Louisbourg National Historic Site and Kejimkujik National Park to introduce interpretive programs, and helped pave the way for the petroglyphs in Kejimkujik and Bedford to receive national recognition as historic sites. "I wouldn't have come to Nova Scotia if I didn't love it," says Sable, who hails from Massachusetts. "I didn't move to Boulder, for example."

Architect David Garrett in 1993 created a remarkable show for the Mary Black Gallery of the Nova Scotia Centre for Craft and Design. His love of Halifax's once dominant street led to *Barrington Street — A Walk Through Time*. Garrett also designed the Dream Home for the 1993 Metro United Way's Dream Home sweepstakes.

Carolyn Gimian, meanwhile, is director of the Vajradhatu Archives in the basement of the Shambhala Centre, and also president of the Council of Nova Scotia Archives, which oversees the province's eighty archives. Gimian represents Nova Scotia at national meetings, and in 1996 was part of the Canadian delegation which attended meetings in China.

Finally, *The Vajradhatu Sun* in 1991 was a twenty-eight-page, black and white tabloid magazine aimed at Buddhists. A year later it changed its name, shape, and outlook. Today, *Shambhala Sun* is a seventy-eight page, full colour, values-based publication. Available on newsstands throughout Canada and the U.S., it sells an average of 18,000 copies per issue.

* * *

Education

Rarely does independent research earn national media attention. Yet Barbara Blouin's 1992 study of municipal welfare practices in Nova Scotia made headlines across Canada. Unequal municipal practices, Blouin said, broke the federal-provincial agreement on social assistance. As well as national acclaim, her efforts earned her the Progress Women of Excellence Award presented by the Halifax-Cornwallis chapter of the Canadian Progress Club.

Blouin has since founded the Inheritance Project. Its aim is to have people with inherited wealth talk about the guilt and confusion inherent in that situation. As a first step, she co-authored *The Legacy of Inherited Wealth* (1995, Trio Press).

"The biggest myth going is that money makes you happy. It's just not true," Blouin says. " At the same time, there's nothing positive about poverty... More and more I think of money as something essentially neutral — as neither good nor bad. It's the attitude you have to money that's important, especially your own money.

"Money can be a means of having a lot of power over other people; it can be used in negative ways. Or it can be used to fulfill oneself and other people, and for doing positive things in the community."

Kay Crinean is on the cutting edge of communication technology. The executive director of NovaKnowledge, she used to work for the National Development Economic Office in London. On arrival in Nova Scotia she started working on economic development issues for the provincial government, specializing in information technology. But when she heard about the fledgling non-profit association, she jumped to lead NovaKnowledge. Its purpose is to promote the development of a knowledge-based economy in Nova Scotia.

"This province has everything it needs to do well in the new economy," Crinean says. "We have lots of educated people, which is the raw material, plus the technology that enables us to reach out to the world. We have to stop thinking, 'You can't do that here, you have to be somwhere else.'"

The organization has 400 members, half from the business sector and one-quarter from government. It is financed by corporations, government, and members.

"Our message is: some mainstays of the economy here are declining, but we have new opportunities. We have to work together, and work hard, to seize the opportunities, and we have to understand how to do it. Instead of feeling unempowered we have to get off our butts. We are addressing the habitual pattern of holding out a begging bowl to the government to save us. They can't do that any more."

NovaKnowledge holds two conferences a year to bring together Nova Scotians who share a desire to provide the province with a strong place in the information age. It produces a newsletter and home page to talk about opportunities. It also collects old corporate and government computers and gives them to schools. So far, more than 3,000 have been provided. When Industry Canada heard of this program, it initiated a similar process nationwide. NovaKnowledge won an Industry Canada award for the most innovative program to put computers in Canadian schools.

Crinean says that the most important thing NovaKnowledge is doing is basically "economic Shambhala Training, because the fundamental point everyone comes back to is 'Our attitude is the biggest obstacle.' If we could change it from 'We can't do it,' we'd have everything we need. So we spend a lot of time on changing attitude."

Men for Change was formed by a group of Nova Scotia men after the 1989 Montreal Massacre, in which a deranged young man murdered fourteen women. In 1991 sangha member Andrew Safer joined, and became one of three Men for Change members to write a school program. The curriculum was ready in April 1994, and in the first six months was picked up by school boards, youth centres, transition houses, government departments, and conflict resolution centres in Ontario, Quebec, Saskatchewan, B.C., Alberta, Newfoundland, Yukon, the Northwest Territories, Colorado, and Pennsylvania. Since that time it has spread to be accepted in even more jurisdictions, including Nova Scotia. Any school board in the province is now free to use the program.

It's devised to teach kids to treat each other, and themselves, with respect. There are lessons for three grades. The grade 7 program focuses on Dealing with Aggression, grade 8 considers Gender Equality and Media Awareness, and grade 9 with Forming Healthy Relationships.

"It's a sad fact this sort of thing is very, very needed," said Mike Law, vice-principal of Beechville-Lakeside and Timberlea schools. "One thing this Men for Change material does that others don't is it takes a look at beliefs and attitudes, the reasons we have some of those."

There are two Shambhala schools in Halifax: an elementary school for grades primary through four, and a middle school for grades five through ten. Founded by sangha members, they remain independently owned and not officially associated with Shambhala International.

Shambhala Middle School opened with twenty-five kids in 1993. Principal Jane Hester was among a group of twelve parents who established the Middle School. A teacher with twenty years experience, Hester decided she didn't want her thirteen-year-old entering a regular junior high school. From an original home on Harvard Street, the Middle School has since moved to the former Alexander MacKay School, on Russell Street in the north end. In every grade subjects include French, art, music, physical education, history, and literature or language arts. In grade nine and ten optional classes include alternative health, drama, creative writing, and massage. Students and teacher sit in a circle and meditate to start and end each day, and a biweekly talk circle gives everyone a chance to speak. Fifty-two students and seven teachers are enrolled. Tuition is $4,000 per student; the school receives no public funding.

The Shambhala Elementary School is younger and smaller, and for younger, smaller kids. Twenty-five children attended grades primary through four in 1995-96, and were instructed by three teachers. The school can be found on the third floor of Veith House, in the north end. Founded by a group of concerned parents, it opened in 1994. Shambhala Elementary uses the Enki

Curriculum, developed for the school by Beth Sutton, a sangha member in Lexington, Mass. Every subject is taught through storytelling, painting, movement, and singing. "For math I introduce four gnomes: Mr. Plus, Mr. Minus, Mr. Times, and Mr. Divide," says grade one teacher Christine Lohry. "The quality of what they are learning sinks in. By the time they go to pen and paper it's in their system, it's not an abstract thing."

No meditation is taught to children this young, but meditative arts including flower arranging and kudo are practiced. Rather than focusing solely on Canadian or Western culture, stories from a cross-section of world cultures are told.

"These children came from public schools, and after three months it was amazing how they had opened up," says board member Jackie Mitchell. "They smile, they talk to adults instead of cowering. They just love school — every single one of them. It's what you wished you had as a child."

Tuition is $2,800 for half-day primary students, and $3,800 for full-day grades one through four.

* * *

Enterprises

Sangha members were instrumental in bringing to Halifax a community-based alternative to banking — peer lending, which is geared to help small businesses. Since being established by a Toronto couple in 1983, non-profit Calmeadow Peer Lending has branched out across the nation, overseeing loans of more than $1 million. In Halifax Andy and Wendy Carr, Paul Susnis, Jan Watson, and John Odenthal were among the people who contacted Calmeadow, and worked to create a local branch. They called it Shambhala Peer Lending; the name has since been changed to Calmeadow Halifax. The group hired sangha member Connie Berman as the part-time, paid co-ordinator of the fund. Non-sangha members are welcome: board members include Spots Pots owner Sue Klabunde and provincial NDP leadership candidate Yvonne Atwell.

Also working to improve the state of the Nova Scotia economy are Alan Sloan and John Odenthal. Odenthal is a policy analyst with the provincial Economic Renewal Agency. Sloan is executive director of the Western Valley Development Authority. Based in Bridgetown, it's a non-profit society working to develop the Annapolis Valley.

Not all sangha enterprises have been successful. A few stores were short-lived, and there was one disaster.

Maritime Capital Investments Ltd. was an ambitious Halifax development company in the 1980s. It renovated historic buildings including Halliburton House (still considered among the city's best small hotels), a number of houses on Bland Street, and the Knightsbridge condominiums on Inglis. It also built the row houses on Bauer Street. In 1989, however, Maritime Capital died. The National Trust Company, Montreal Trust, Prenor Trust, CIBC, and Lloyd's Bank all filed suits for mortgage defaults on properties. The next year, the properties went on the auction block and were reclaimed by those financial institutions. More than two million dollars was lost, most of it borrowed from Martha Bonzi. At the time of its collapse Maritime Capital was owned by three people, all sangha members. One, Jim Drescher, was forced to declare personal bankruptcy.

"I felt badly that people lost money or were hurt in any way by this situation," Drescher says, "and it was terribly embarrassing to go bankrupt myself. I now see that as a part of my life that was tangential. I was in forestry before, then got into the development business, and am back in forestry now."

Drescher has a Masters degree in Ecology; his wife Margaret a degree in Ornamental Horticulture. After the collapse of Maritime Capital they left metro for New Germany, Lunenburg County, where they opened organic Windhorse Farm. Two years ago they also began The Ecoforestry School in the Maritimes. It's one of only two schools in North America granting certificates in ecoforestry.

Sangha members are playing a major role in the rise of organic farming in Nova Scotia, operating four farms. Besides the Dreschers, Stephanie Garrett-Greenberg and David Greenberg grow the summer crops of Norland Farm near Wolfville; Pam and Alex De Nicola own Highland Farm near Windsor; and David and Nancy Roberts own Four Seasons Farm in Maitland.

Each of the farms have their specialties; the Roberts' sell much of their produce to restaurants and hotels, including the government-owned Digby Pines and Keltic Lodge. Their harvest consists of eighteen culinary herbs, and vegetables including golden beets. "The reason we got into farming was that eighty-five per cent of the vegetables sold in Nova Scotia are imported from the U.S.," David Roberts said. "Chefs like what we offer because it doesn't have to be shipped so far."

Ed Hanczaryk, meanwhile, is a golf professional with a distinctly Shambhalian perspective. He is the only golf pro in Nova Scotia whose business card refers to how well you play when your mind is fully engaged.

Chapter 11

Enlightened Society

Most Shambhala community members paste a small sticker to their car bumpers or house doors. It shows two blue and two gold waves curling into each other in a stylized yin/yang motif. His Holiness the Karmapa, head of one of the four schools of Tibetan Buddhism, created the design specifically for the community — after seeing it in a dream. Today it's commonly known as the dream flag, and can be seen on buttons, flags, and stickers.

Other bumper stickers would be appropriate. "I'd Rather Be Meditating." "My Other Vehicle is a Mahayana." "I Breathe, Therefore I Am." "Buddhists Do It With Their Minds." "This Bud's For You." But the preferred sticker, appropriately, is one with no words. It follows the Buddhist and Shambhala teachings that reality exists on a level deeper than language, beyond what any concept can reach.

Some Nova Scotians would not be impressed with this. There are people in the province who think it's fitting that the first syllable in the community name is "Sham." Most, however, have in the past twenty years moved from suspicion to skepticism to an acceptance that the Shambhala community is here to stay, and has honourable intentions. This acceptance ranges from lukewarm to a full embrace.

Chogyam Trungpa did not aim for all Nova Scotians to join the Shambhala sangha. He chose the province because he wanted a safe place for Tibetan Buddhist and Shambhala wisdom to survive and continue. He picked Nova Scotia for cultural and geographical reasons and, most importantly, because of the character of the people. Some Nova Scotians will, naturally, become interested in Shambhala Training, Buddhism, or the Nalanda meditative arts, but in a sense those people are gravy. Trungpa chose Nova Scotia more because of the quality of the people who would *not* be interested in meditation, but would accept a meditative community joining this society.

So far, it's benefitted both parties.

"Those people who moved up to Nova Scotia are much harder to do business with now," Alyn Lyon says. "They are nicer than they used to be, have slowed down a lot. They are a lot less American."

Lyon, director of the Rocky Mountain Shambhala Centre in Colorado, says this with a smile. A desire to be less aggressive, to treat life as something more than business, is part of the reason the Shambhala community moved to Nova Scotia. Both the people who moved and the ones who stayed in Colorado — each community numbers just over 500 — agree it's working. They say the less savoury aspects of American culture are being rubbed away, leaving people less gruff, less money-centred, and in less of a hurry. The newcomers are also now past the transition stage, are planting roots and becoming Canadian citizens. They are becoming Nova Scotians, too — are learning to love fiddle music and stand in the kitchen at parties.

Not all sangha members, of course, are learning from their home province. Some continue to be strangers in a strange land. A minority of the Shambhala community regards Nova Scotian culture the way many people see museums — as quaint and interesting, but not particularly relevant. They find local habits charming — in the fact drivers almost always stop for pedestrians, for example — but don't allow themselves to be changed by the wisdom of the place.

Overall, however, the Shambhala community has been greatly affected by their move. They came looking for a corner of North America where materialism has not destroyed profound values, where modern and traditional influences exist in a meaningful balance. After some difficult times getting used to the weather and pace, and building or finding niches in the provincial economy, most are delighted with the change.

The move has been good for Nova Scotia, too. What region would not want an influx of bright, educated, caring people who abhor proselytization and respect local traditions? Sangha members have founded and developed scores of businesses and organizations that are working to make the province a better place to live. Rubbing shoulders with the Shambhala community — an energetic and confident bunch — has helped the provincial self-esteem. It's also helped Nova Scotians articulate what is so special about the province. (All Nova Scotians know the place is magical, but sometimes need someone else to point this out.) The main effect of the sangha presence is this: it has helped the province's entrenched fatalism make room for hope.

What will the Shambhala community look like twenty, fifty, or a hundred years from now? Indications are it will become less and less a separate entity, and its members will regard their practices more as a way of life and less as their identity.

"Is this something Nova Scotians are interested in? That Nova Scotians can hear? So far, it looks very good," Halifax Shambhala Training Director David Burkholder says. "I think the Nova Scotians who are involved are going to do a lot more with it than their American counterparts. They're making it a way of life, without seeing themselves as separate. They don't get this and then think, 'This makes us Shambhala, separate from other people.' It's just a way of creating a lot of energy and enthusiasm, and going deeper into their own life and experience."

At some point, all members hit a plateau where the practice becomes routine, Richard John says. At that point they have to choose: they can either quit, or choose to reignite it. If the latter is chosen two routes are open: a devout, religious approach, or a worldly approach. The latter, he says, "You can do in terms of your home, your family, relationships, work, the way you relate to money, education, and community. Within all of these ordinary things, there really is the path. A path connecting with basic goodness, and still part of a meditation path. It's what Trungpa Rinpoche called meditation in action.

"People usually want to gravitate to one or the other, they want to be more Buddhist, or more Shambhalian. But I think the most characteristic thing about Trungpa's teaching, and this community, is this dual path. The idea of the two appoaches. You can do it in the world, yet you still have to have a profound practice. Or you can go deeply into meditation practice, but still have to relate to the world. Those things keep each other out of trouble."

* * *

Outside of tulkus, this book does not deal with the question of reincarnation. While probably the best-known and most-misunderstood Buddhist concept in the Western World, Trungpa only rarely talked about reincarnation. He wanted to cut Westerners' fascination with it, and talk about more immediate concerns. Similarly, in Rick Fields' remarkable history of Buddhism in the U.S., *How the Swans Came to the Lake* (Shambhala Publications), the word reincarnation does not even appear in the index.

Sangha members have a wide variety of feelings on the subject. Some believe in tulkus literally: a child proclaimed a tulku is the incarnation of a previous person. Most, however, follow Trungpa's suggestion that tulkus are not to be taken literally, and that the choosing of tulkus is greatly affected by many things, not least of all politics.

Paradoxical to the end, Trungpa did, however, make comments about his own next rebirth. He told a number of his closest aides that he would only be with them for twenty years (he was close, dying after seventeen) and would come back in Japan. Again, there is debate as to how serious he was in these predictions.

If he was serious about Japan, he was off by several thousand kilometres. The Twelfth Trungpa Tulku is alive and well and living in Tibet. He is Trungpa Chokyi Sengay XII, a little boy six years old. Although it has been known for several years that the child is proclaimed Trungpa's incarnation, the Shambhala leadership has declined to become deeply involved. The principal concern is that paying attention to the child would distract from more immediate, down-to-earth questions.

* * *

No matter how the Shambhala community evolves in Nova Scotia, at its heart will be meditation. Could meditation ever be accepted as normal, rather than exotic, in the province? It has a great deal of baggage to overcome: the word is widely thought to indicate something foreign and mind-wasting, religious and bizarre. Meditation has only slightly more credibility than levitation.

Nova Scotians may enjoy a less-hectic way of life than most people in the Western World, but the speed of life everywhere is quickening. If Nova Scotians want to protect their sanity in increasingly crazy times, they will have to do something. The fact that thousands of people in the province already meditate means the idea of "sitting" is less foreign in Nova Scotia than in, say, Minnesota or Montreal. So while it's not possible to imagine the entire population meditating, it is conceivable that those who do will not be considered unusual.

Could I make meditation an integral part of my life? The Buddhist aim of moving closer and closer to ultimate reality attracts me but, shallow as it may sound, there are other things I'd rather do with my time. Investing half-an-hour a day to enhance the other twenty-three-and-a-half, however, makes perfect sense. Of course a daily practice is too demanding, but practicing two or three times a week seems entirely plausible.

In theory.

Maybe.

Reality sets in; excuses can always be found. As much as I think meditation has value and makes sense, I can't swear it will be one of my life's permanent features. Interestingly, though, every time a couple of weeks lapses, I find myself go back. It's a sure way to lessen the noise of the mind.

While it's conceivable more and more Nova Scotians discover the benefits of meditation, it is hard to imagine Nova Scotians flocking to identify with the Shambhala flag. While joining a community is an attraction for some, for others it's the greatest obstacle preventing them from taking Shambhala levels or Buddhist meditation classes. There's a fear of changing identity, of having to join a group and lifestyle.

Is this fear justified? These are legitimate practices; brainwashing is not being offered. Certainly thousands of people have benefitted by studying the Shambhala teachings, and millions from Buddhism and meditation. The higher levels of vajrayana Buddhism, however, while immeasurably rewarding can also be dangerous, and should be avoided by anyone not willing to put their mind on the line.

Cape Breton is guaranteed to become more and more important in the Shambhala future. If Trungpa considered Nova Scotia "a sacred place," his feelings for Cape Breton were off the scale. His first trip to the province was going poorly — until the minute he crossed the causeway. He placed the sangha's only monastery — Gampo Abbey — near the northern tip of the island. And just north of Cape Smokey, right at the bottom of the long road coming down the mountain, is a special valley. Trungpa loved this valley the first time he saw it. Here, he said, is the perfect place for Kalapa. In the legendary kingdom of Shambhala, Kalapa was the capital city.

A couple of years ago the valley came up for sale and sangha members bought it, renaming it the Kalapa Valley. No money is at hand and no plans are in the works, but in the future...

If the Shambhala community and greater Nova Scotian society are to mix strengths and work together in the future, tendencies must be overcome. Xenophobia on the part of longtime Nova Scotians, and closemindedness on the part of the sangha.

175

The Shambhala community is ordinarily accepted today, but then it has been twenty years, they speak English, and are almost all white. These are ugly reasons to accept someone. If the sangha experiences any more growing pains, it will have to hope Nova Scotians have progressed to the point where they don't turn and run. There can be a thin line between hospitality and hostility. Many sangha members, meanwhile, have a hard time believing that anyone who drinks Big 8 pop can be as enlightened as people who prefer ginseng tea. This attitude alienates many potential friends.

The Shambhala community came all this way to build an enlightened society. Like so much of what Chogyam Trungpa said, this can be heard on many levels. Some sangha members believe he was referring solely to Shambhala community aspirations. Others think he was predicting the result of old and new Nova Scotians working together to create a better province. It's up to each of us.

Chapter 12

Afterthoughts

"Since its arrival in Nova Scotia the Buddhist community has contributed enormously to our province. It's hard to imagine Nova Scotia without them. We enjoy a great diversity of new establishments which have enhanced our capital city, and we have superb new private schools. We benefit from the Buddhist community's approach to life, which is both worldly and spiritual. How lucky for us that they chose to come here."

— *John Savage, Premier of Nova Scotia*

"I'm pleased they're here. You sometimes look at religious groups with concern, but these are real down-to-earth people. People who take an interest in basic community functions, like schools."

— *Walter Fitzgerald, Mayor of Halifax*

"The city looks better because they are here. Their reconstruction of properties has class, is a nice type of architecture. The centre on Tower Road is a good example — I was familiar with it because I belong to the Knights of Columbus. When that building was a Knights of Columbus Hall it was a bad design and poorly used. They were very creative in what they did — they made an attractive building out of one that was unattractive. What that has to do with religion is a good question. However, it shows creativity."

— *Ron Wallace, Halifax mayor 1980–91*

"Life is not a problem to solve, it is a reality to experience."

— *The Buddha*

"When the Iron Bird flies and horses run on wheels, Tibetans will be scattered like ants across the world..."
— *Milarepa, 11th century Tibetan Buddist saint*

"You should examine yourself and ask how many times you have tried to connect with your heart, fully and truly."
— *Trungpa Rinpoche*

"Buddhism has a gigantic amount of cultural and religious and philisophical baggage that has accumulated over 2,500 years. But the Buddha was much more like a Shambhala person than a Buddhist. I mean, he wasn't a Buddhist."
— *Halifax sangha member Richard John*

"At a talk at the Lord Nelson Hotel a woman asked Trungpa Rinpoche, 'What if you don't like to sit?' He said to her, 'Do you have a daughter?' And the woman would not answer. So he asked again, 'Do you have a daughter?' He might have repeated himself half a dozen times. And finally he said, 'Well, then! Do you want your daughter to grow up like you did? That is why you sit. If you think you sit for yourself, that's absolutely wicked. You sit for other people.'"
— *Halifax Shambhala Training director David Burkholder*

"We are not talking about philosophy, but we are talking about how on earth, how in the name of heaven and earth, we can actually become decent human beings without trying to entertain ourselves from here to the next corner."
— *Trungpa Rinpoche*

"Basketball is a complex dance that requires shifting from one objective to another at lightning speed... the secret is not thinking. That doesn't mean being stupid; it means quieting the endless jabbering of thoughts so that your body can do instinctively what it's been trained to do without the mind getting in the way."
— *Chicago Bulls' coach Phil Jackson, in* Sacred Hoops: Spiritual Lessons of a Hardwood Warrior *(Hyperion, New York, 1995)*

178

"In the name of heaven and earth, you can afford to make love to yourself."

— *Trungpa Rinpoche*

"Really, Halifax is a pretty hopeless place. It has a harbour. It used to have a good university. You don't intend to stay there indefinitely, do you?"

— *Wain talking to Murray in Hugh MacLennan's*
Barometer Rising *(Macmillan)*

"Trungpa Rinpoche had a deep respect for and tremendous interest in the people of Nova Scotia. He didn't say, 'Here's a convenient place where no one will bother us.' It was a positive draw."

— *Halifax sangha member Michael Scott*

"Wherever it's gone, Buddhism has taken indigenous practices and cultures and incorporated them. Flavors are being added all along the way. We don't know what Buddhism will be fifty years from now. We don't know what Shambhala will be. We know what dignity is; we know what sanity is. But we don't know how they will manifest fifty years from now."

— *Halifax sangha member Barry Boyce*

"Shambhala vision is not purely a philosophy... It is learning to treat yourself better, so that you can help to build an enlightened society."

— *Trungpa Rinpoche*

"Do I miss God? Well, I never encountered Him — it would be hard to miss Him. I never noticed there was anybody out there who would come to my rescue when I got in trouble. It had to be me doing it. 'God helps the one who helps himself' is basically what I grew up with. Buddhists don't believe there is a God — you have to do the doing yourself. Which is exactly what I've always felt."

— *Maine sangha member Martha Bonzi*

"Every day people are straying from the church and going back to God."

— *Lenny Bruce*

"A normal human being does not want the Kingdom of Heaven: he wants life on earth to continue. This is not solely because he is 'weak,' 'sinful' and anxious for a 'good time.' Most people get a fair amount of fun out of their lives, but on balance life is suffering, and only the very young or the very foolish imagine otherwise. Ultimately it is the Christian attitude which is self-interested and hedonistic, since the aim is always to get away from the painful struggle of earthly life and find eternal peace in some kind of Heaven or Nirvana. The humanist attitude is that the struggle must continue and that death is the price of life."

— *George Orwell,* Inside the Whale and Other Essays *(Penguin Books)*

"The truth that many people never understand, until it is too late, is that the more you try to avoid suffering the more you suffer because smaller and more insignificant things begin to torture you in proportion to your fear of being hurt."

—*Thomas Merton*

"The root of fear is believing in oneself too much, which makes oneself very vulnerable... Cheerfulness, a sense of humour, is the starting point. And then not holding onto oneself too much is the second point."

— *Trungpa Rinpoche*

"People are black and white in their perceptions around Trungpa Rinpoche. Which is funny, because he didn't have a dualistic view of the world."

— *Halifax sangha member Lesley Ann Patten*

"The real meaning of wealth is knowing how to create a godlike situation in your life."

— *Trungpa Rinpoche*

"It is through having experienced all experience that the soul finally achieves perfect sympathy and understanding."

— *Philosopher Joseph Campbell*

"In Buddhism, compassion often leads to a completely passive state which I do not agree with."

— *Khandro Rinpoche, Abbess of Rumtek Monastery in Sikkim*

"Trungpa Rinpoche always said, 'It's a kitchen sink reality.' We were looking for some trip to save us, but he was always bringing us back down to, 'It's the things right in front of you. It's your world. It's your everyday world.'"

— *Halifax sangha member Barry Boyce*

"This place is owned by Buddhists?"

— *Coffee drinker at the Trident Cafe*

"(Trungpa Rinpoche) gave us many things, and now he has given us Gyepe Dorje (Sakyong Mipham Rinpoche)."

— *Penor Rinpoche, Supreme Head of the Nyingma Lineage*

"Compassion is the ground of enlightenment."

— *Sakyong Mipham Rinpoche*

"Within our lifetime there will be great problems in the world, but let us make sure that within our lifetime no disasters happen. We can prevent them. It is up to us. We can save the world from destruction, to begin with. That is why Shambhala vision exists. It is a centuries-old idea: by serving this world, we can save it. But saving the world is not enough. We have to work to build an enlightened human society as well."

— *Trungpa Rinpoche*

"Personally, I think a lot of people feel a growing trust in the sakyong. I'm sure he has and will make mistakes. But so what? I trust they are not going to be disastrous."

— *Halifax sangha member Michael Scott*

"Being tidy is the Buddhist message, always."

— *Trungpa Rinpoche*

Chogyam Trungpa wrote hundreds of poems, including several concerning his choice of Nova Scotia as world headquarters for the Shambhala community. Here are a few of particular interest.

Whycocomagh?

Sometimes there are trees;
Sometimes there are rocks;
However, occasionally there are lakes;
Always, to be sure, there are houses;
To be sure certain there are views of a certain gentleman being
    crucified.
Nevertheless, the deep-fried food is very decent,
So good that one almost forgets bourgeois cuisine.

The coastal sky seems to frown at us
With its benevolent threat;
We receive plentiful rain.
In green valley pastures brown cows graze.
Tibetan-tea-like rough rivers carry the highland soil.
Occasional mist and fog bring wondrous possibilities.
Naive hitchhikers laugh and scrutinize our convoy.
The highlands are beautiful, free from pollution,
The lowlands regular, telling the whole truth:
There is nothing to hide.
Harmonious province hangs together,
But for occasional economic panic.
Men of Shambhala would feel comfortable and confident in the
    province of no big deal,
Flying the banner of St. Andrew adorned with the lion of Scotland,
    red and yellow.
We find it beyond conflict to fly the banner of the Great Eastern Sun.

It is curious to see their flags strung on yellow cords;
Nice to watch the children cycling in the ditch;
Nice to discover all the waiters serving on their first day;
Nice to see that nobody is apologetic;
Good to see alders taking root after the forest fire of pines.

June 1977, New Glasgow, Nova Scotia

Farewell to Boulder

It was Karma Dzong,
It was full moon,
It was sunshine,
It was Karma Dzong—
The way the sun shines
And the way the moon eclipses,
The way the tortilla is shaped,
The way the curries taste,
The way the Mataam Fez operates,
The way the Kobe An executes,
The way the Karma Dzong operates,
The way the sun shines in Boulder,
The way the people smile in Boulder,
The way the real estate operates,
The way the men work,
The way the women feel,
The way sexuality is handled.

It is time for us to change to a new planet,
Fresh planet,
Extra planet.
It is time for us to go elsewhere,
Where donkeys can talk,
Horses can play,
Dogs can run.
It is time to go where sunshine is not all that frequent,
It is time to avoid the Flatirons,
It is time to avoid ponderosa,
It is time to come closer to the ocean,
It is time to take pride in the small island,
It is time to be small,
It is not time to be big,
It is time to be modest,
It is time to eat fish as opposed to meat,
It is time to move to Nova Scotia,

It is time to enjoy the crescent moon, at least a croissant!
It is time to be a human being.
It is time to *be*.
Be in Nova Scotia,
Be in little island,
Be in fresh air.
Let us be natural,
Let us not ask any questions,
Let us drop all the questions,
Let us be,
Be, be, be.

Hail to the discovery!
We have discovered something very ordinary
But we have experienced something extraordinary.
Let us be,
Let us discover,
Let us celebrate,
Let us appreciate,
Let us celebrate that we have discovered insignificant island,
Let us appreciate the ordinariness of it,
Let us celebrate!

October 25, 1982, Halifax

Halifax

Big roll by the thunder,
Big speech by the lion,
Lovely maple trees making their statements:
I love this world,
I hate this world,
Too demanding,
Too kind,
Basically not giving any reference point.
Roar like a rock mountain,
Laugh like a giant waterfall,
Cry like a peacock's mate—
Who is kidding who?
Success is in the palm of your hand,
Doubt is missing a flea on your hips.
Be gentle and kind,
Don't give an inch,
Your inscrutability is mine—
Let us meet together in Cape Breton.

October 19, 1977, Charlemont, Mass.

Merrier than the Maritimes

Nova Scotia as seen at its best:
How the earth and sky can relate with mist and rain and the frustrations
    of fishermen.
Cape Forchu at Yarmouth brings us eye-opening possibilities of Pembroke
    Shore,
Kelly Cove introduces us into Darling Lake,
As we reach Port Maitland we discover the possiblities of Cape St. Mary
    which brings us to
      Meteghan River,
By way of Bay of Fundy we find ourselves in Digby,
As we approach further, we find ourselves realizing Port George,
As we begin to look forward to Cape Split,
Our journey goes further:
How should we enter into the country –
Whether it should be by way of Cape Blomidon or elsewhere –
Evangeline Beach is tempting –
But should we ride on a horse to conquer Dartmouth across land –
Or should we sail around by way of Cape Sable –
We are inspired to be in Halifax;
Gentlemen from Cape Haven might have something to say about our trip
    altogether,
As we sweep across the peninsula,
We find ourselves cultivating Cape Capstan,
And cutting the tie with the mainland at Amherst,
Including pylons and electrical systems and all the rest of it;
As we reach Heather Beach,
We might be tempted to be in Fox Harbour,
The eastern sunrise becomes questionable at that point:
Whether we have eastern sunrise or not,
Our only reference point is Pictou,
Where we stayed before:
There the land and heaven are joined together,
Seemingly we enjoyed ourselves;
New Glasgow is a fantastic area,
As to relating with luscious earth,

As to bringing general prosperous outlook overcoming industrialism,
We are attracted to Cape George;
Depth of the earth could be brought out by means of Big Marsh,
Local vision can be brought together in the County of Antigonish,
By working together with Guysborough County,
So we have a chance to bring together the mainland and build big city,
In the name of Pictou-Guysborough,
We could invite any potential prosperous and elegant situation as possible
    London, Paris,
     Rome blah blah blah;
The county of Inverness,
We will continue to the top point of Cape St. Lawrence,
We will build high point of sane society,
With the courtesy of Victoria County, Keltic Lodge and Ingonish are
    included,
Thus we go further:
In County of Cape Breton we raise the morale of Sydney,
With the help of Richmond County,
The total vision of Nova Scotia should be based on Capital of Sydney.
When Sydney is raised to its highest level,
The rest of the peninsula can be brought up at its best.
Thus we partly conquer the Atlantic Ocean.
Victory to the true command.
Take pride in our peninsula.

November 29, 1980, Keltic Lodge,
Ingonish, Cape Breton

Afterthought

Such a precious human body,
Difficult to rediscover;
Such precious pain,
Not difficult to discover;
Such an old story
Is by now a familiar joke.
You and I know the facts and the case history;
We have a mutual understanding of each other
Which has never been sold or bought by anyone.
Our mutual understanding keeps the thread of sanity.
Sometimes the thread is electrified,
Sometimes it is smeared with honey and butter;
Nevertheless, we have no regrets.
Since I am here,
Seemingly you are here too.
Let us practice!
Sitting is a jewel that ornaments our precious life.

March 21, 1978